EMMA

Volume 1

By Kaoru Mori

-Contents-

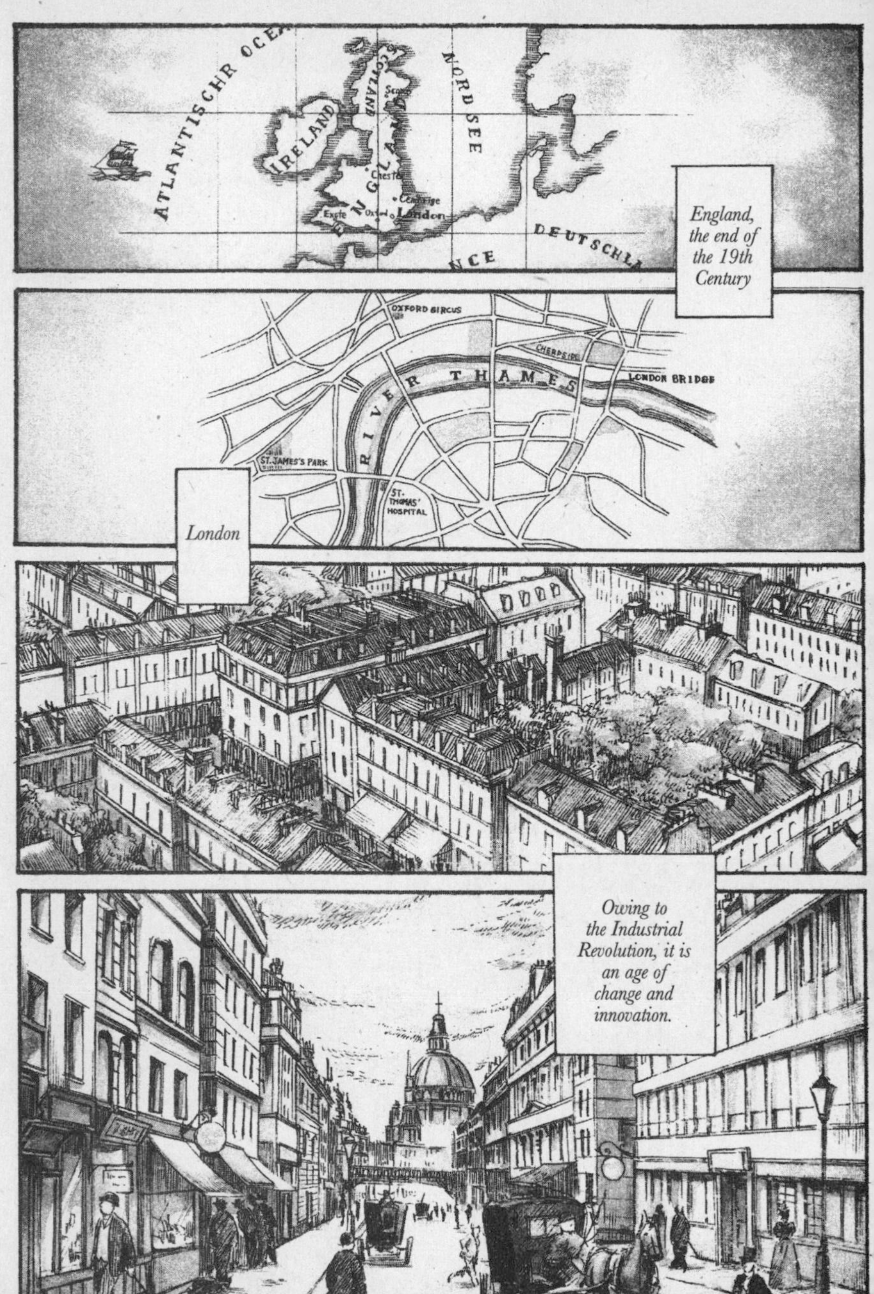
IRELAND
NORD SEE
London
England, the end of the 19th Century
OXFORD CIRCUS
CHEAPSIDE
RIVER THAMES
LONDON BRIDGE
ST. JAMES'S PARK
ST. THOMAS' HOSPITAL
London
Owing to the Industrial Revolution, it is an age of change and innovation.

And yet...
...it is also an age when traditional lifestyles and a class system remain entrenched in society...
...and horse-drawn carriages still have the run of the road.
CHAPTER 1: THE VISITOR

WE'RE *HERE,* GUV'NOR.

MM... OH. THANK YOU.

I'M ALWAYS AROUND THESE PARTS, SO JUST WHISTLE IF YOU NEED ME.

29

BUMP

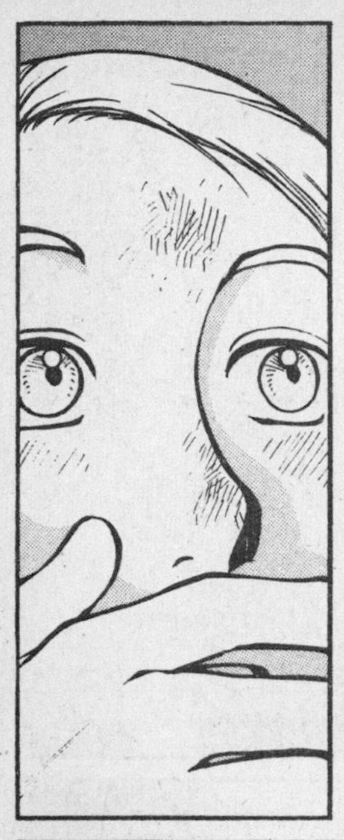

I'M SORRY! ARE YOU ALL RIGHT?!
I HAD NO IDEA SOMEONE WOULD BE STANDING THERE!!

EMMA? WHAT'S THE MATTER?

AH...YES, THAT'S ALL RIGHT. I'M PERFECTLY FINE.
I AM REALLY SO SORRY!

AH! YOUR HAT!

IT'S BEEN A LONG TIME, MADAM.
IT'S ME, WILLIAM JONES.

...WELL, I'LL BE. YES IT CERTAINLY HAS BEEN A LONG TIME.
YOUV'E GOTTEN A LOT BIGGER.

AH!

BUT THAT'S PECULIAR...I SEEM TO RECALL YOU AS HAVING A SLIGHTLY MORE *HANDSOME* FACE.
UM, I BELIEVE THAT'S DUE TO JUST BEFORE ...

I'VE MENTIONED TO YOU BEFORE, HAVEN'T I, EMMA, THAT I WAS A LIVE-IN GOVERNESS A LONG TIME AGO?
FOR THIS YOUNG MAN.
OH.

HO-HO-HO! STANDING IN FRONT OF AN OPENING DOOR. A WONDERFUL EXAMPLE OF BEING IN THE WRONG PLACE AT THE WRONG TIME!
THAT'S JUST LIKE YOU!
......

I'VE ASKED HIM TO COME OVER FOR A VISIT MANY TIMES, BUT HE NEVER HAS.
THANK YOU.
SO I'VE BEEN LEFT IN THE DARK AS TO THE STATE OF YOUR FAMILY.

ONE WOULD THINK THAT FOR SOMEONE WHO PRACTICALLY RAISED YOU FOR FOUR YEARS OF YOUR LIFE, I SHOULD HAVE THE OPPORTUNITY TO SEE YOU A LITTLE MORE OFTEN.

AT THE TIME, THE JONES FAMILY WAS QUITE PROMINENT. I DON'T KNOW HOW THEY FARE NOW, THOUGH.
BUT SEEING YOU BRINGS BACK MEMORIES. HOW IS YOUR FATHER? IS HE WELL?
UM, YES. VERY WELL, THANK YOU.

BY THE WAY, HAVE YOU GOTTEN OVER YOUR BED-WETTING PROBLEM...
...YOUNG MASTER?
PFFFT

...YES. QUITE SOME TIME AGO, AS A MATTER OF FACT.
I SEE.
WELL, THAT'S GOOD TO HEAR.

AH, EMMA!
OPEN THE CURTAINS, WOULD YOU?
YES, MA'AM.

OH, THAT'S RIGHT. YOU HAVE A VERITABLE ARMY OF THEM AT YOUR HOME.
I REMEMBER THEY WOULD DO EVERYTHING FOR YOU, FROM DRESSING YOU TO LORD WHO KNOWS WHAT ELSE!

ARE MAIDS SUCH *RARE* CREATURES FOR YOU?
AH!
NO...
I...

SLAM

I THOUGHT YOU WOULD HAVE CHANGED MORE IN TEN YEARS...
BRRRING
BRRRING
THE TELE-PHONE.
WAIT RIGHT HERE.
OH, I'LL...
THAT'S ALL RIGHT.
IT'S PROBABLY MR. GRAHAM.

SHE'S NOT GOING EASY ON YOU, IS SHE?

CHUCKLE CHUCKLE

SHE USED TO BE *MUCH* SCARIER, THOUGH. MORE SO THAN MY FATHER.

AND *STRICTER* THAN ANYONE I'VE EVER MET.

IF I FORGOT TO DO MY HOMEWORK, SHE WOULD MAKE ME SIT FACING THE WALL FOR AN HOUR TO "PONDER MY MISDEED."

IT WAS WORSE THAN GETTING SCOLDED.

THIS IS ME...

ME, WHEN I WAS 13...

WHEN I TURNED 13, SHE TOOK A PHOTOGRAPH OF ME, AS A "MEMENTO," SHE SAID.
I REMEMBER THAT NOW.
BUT I NEVER THOUGHT THAT PICTURE WOULD WIND UP HERE.

...HUH.

SHE NEVER TOLD YOU ABOUT ME?
NO, NEVER.

?

IT'S FUNNY. I DIDN'T REALIZE THIS WAS *YOU*...

...EVEN THOUGH I MUST HAVE SEEN THE PHOTO EVERY SINGLE DAY.

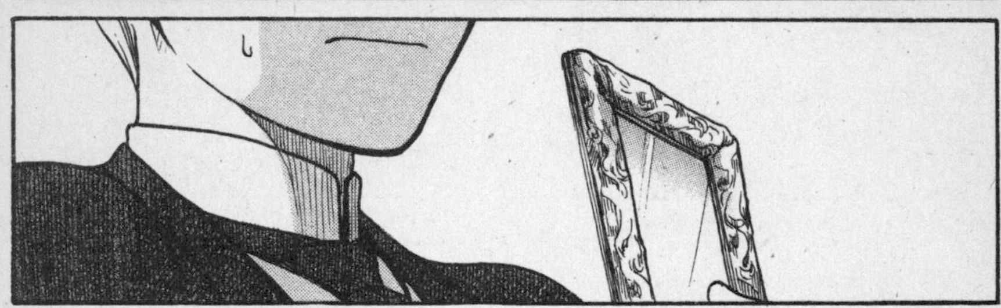

PERHAPS YOU'RE RIGHT. EVEN THOUGH I WAS CONSTANTLY ON THE RECEIVING END OF HER ANGER.
YES, I CAN IMAGINE. BUT THAT'S HER WAY.

SHE PROBABLY THINKS OF YOU AS HER OWN SON.
IF SHE DECORATES THE MANTLE-PIECE WITH YOUR PHOTO...

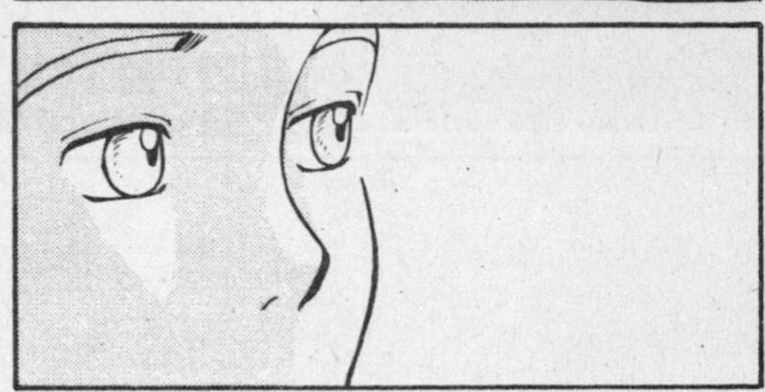

IT WOULD BE NICE IF YOU COULD GET OVER YOUR SENSE OF UNEASE AROUND HER.
QUITE.

OH, UM...
...BY THE WAY...

WOULD YOU BRING ME THAT PACKAGE?
YES, MA'AM.
MR. GRAHAM HAS ARRIVED AT THE STATION, SO I'M OFF TO MEET HIM.
EMMA !!
DO YOU, BY ANY CHANCE, HAVE ANY DAYS OFF...

NEXT TIME, CONTACT ME BEFOREHAND, BY LETTER, SAY, TO LET ME KNOW YOU'RE COMING.
WHEN YOU MEAN TO VISIT A PERSON, IT'S ONLY COMMON SENSE.

YOUR ANSWER?
YES! I WILL!

YES, DO COME AGAIN SOON.
THEN WE CAN SPEND A LEISURELY TIME CATCHING UP ON VARIOUS TOPICS.
......

...I WILL!
GOOD.

...I SHALL SEE YOU AGAIN SOON.
VERY GOOD.

UM, WELL, THEN...

OH!

WHAT IS IT?
IT SEEMS YOUR GUEST HAS FORGOTTEN HIS GLOVES...

HIS GLOVES? OH, HE HASN'T CHANGED A BIT.
HE JUST LEFT, SO IF I HURRY, I CAN...

NO NEED TO BOTHER. HE SAID HE'D COME AGAIN SOON.
AND I'M SURE THAT'S NOT THE ONLY PAIR OF GLOVES HE'S...
......

ON THE OTHER HAND, HE CAN'T HAVE GOTTEN FAR. VERY WELL. WILL YOU DELIVER THESE TO HIM FOR ME?
YES, MA'AM.
I'LL LOCK UP.

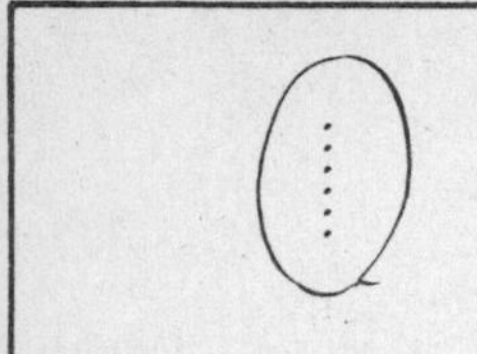
......

HMMM... THE BOY SEEMS TO HAVE USED HIS WILES HERE.
WELL, I'LL TURN A BLIND EYE *THIS TIME.*

AH-CHOO !!

RUB

WE MEET AGAIN, GUV'NOR.
YES, UH... HOW ABOUT THAT?

I'D SAY THAT'S A *UNIQUE* WAY OF WAITING.
OH, DON'T MIND *ME!*

WILL YOU BE NEEDING A RIDE?
NO, I'M FINE. I'M WAITING FOR SOMEONE.

Chapter One:
The End

IN SOCIETY "OFF- SEASON," AS IT IS NOW, THIS IS A FINE PARK TO STROLL THROUGH.
THE SYNDENHAM CRYSTAL PALACE WAS BUILT HERE, FOR THE GREAT EXPOSITION.

...AH. I'M SORRY, I'M HOGGING THE CONVER- SATION.
AM I BORING YOU?

NOT AT ALL.

GOOD.
OF COURSE, I'VE ONLY HEARD STORIES ABOUT THE EXPOSITION...

...BUT THAT BIG ELM TREE BACK THERE? IT WAS SUPPOSED TO BE CUT DOWN. BUT...

...MAYBE WE SHOULD CHANGE THE SUBJECT.
NO, NO.
PLEASE, CONTINUE.

YOUNG MASTER!

YOUNG MASTER!
A PACKAGE HAS COME FOR YOU.

A PACKAGE?

CHAPTER 2: THE GLASSES

SUPERB! IT'S ARRIVED SOONER THAN I EXPECTED!
HAVE YOU ORDERED SOMETHING, YOUNG MASTER?

......

ISN'T IT ABOUT TIME YOU STOPPED REFERRING TO ME AS "YOUNG MASTER?"
I am an adult, you know.
WHAT ARE YOU SAYING?. YOU *ARE* YOUNG MASTER.

WELL, I'LL BE... THIS IS NICELY PUT TOGETHER FOR ITS SIZE.

WHAT'S IT CALLED AGAIN? AN AERO-PLANE?
MM.

TWIST THIS AROUND LIKE SO...

HYAAAA!!
OH!

YOUNG MASTER!!
EHEH HEH. SORRY!
You're faster on your feet than I give you credit for.

OH, YES. THE DELIVERY OF THE PACKAGE MADE ME FORGET TO TELL YOU...
...YOUR FATHER WOULD LIKE TO SEE YOU.

MY FATHER ...
...WHICH MEANS I'M IN FOR A LONG TALK.

WHERE ARE YOU GOING?
FOR A LITTLE WALK.
BUT YOU CAN'T, YOUNG MASTER. YOUR FATHER IS EXPECTING YOU.

YOUNG MASTER !!

HMM...
NO, I BELIEVE THAT WILL DO FOR NOW.

DO YOU NEED ANYTHING ELSE WHILE I'M AT THE STORE?

I'LL BE BACK IN ABOUT TWO HOURS.

TAKE *CARE* OF YOURSELF. EMMA.
YES, MA'AM.

MAYBE I'LL TAKE A WALK TO SEE MISS EMMA.

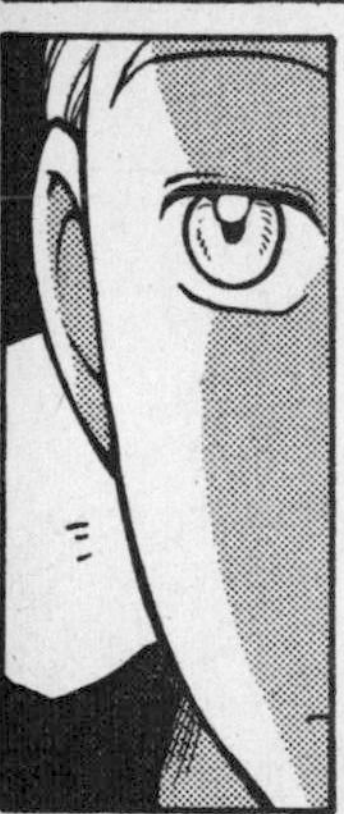

I WISH I COULD JUST RUN INTO HER BY CHANCE...
...BUT WITH MY LUCK, THAT'LL NEVER...

NO, BAD IDEA.
She's too well-guarded...

EH?!
ARE YOU SURE ABOUT THAT?

SIR! THE BILL!

HERE! KEEP THE CHANGE!

MISS EMMA!

......?

!

MR. JONES...!

HELLO ...
...AND GOOD DAY.

I WAS WAVING MY HAND AT YOU FROM THE TIME I WALKED OUT OF THE STORE.
I'M SORRY. I COULDN'T SEE YOU.

DID YOU NOTICE ME BACK THERE?

EVEN THOUGH YOU'RE WEARING GLASSES?
MY EYES HAVE GOTTEN WEAKER AGAIN RECENTLY.

......

WON'T YOU GET NEW GLASSES THEN?
THEY'RE RATHER EXPENSIVE.

I'VE GOT IT! HOW ABOUT I BUY YOU A NEW PAIR AS A PRESENT?!
EH?!

NO, I...I COULDN'T ACCEPT...

OH, PLEASE! WHAT'S ONE PAIR OF GLASSES?

GIVING A PRESENT IS AS NATURAL AS BIRDS FLYING...
...OR CATS WALKING...
...OR CHILDREN FALLING DOWN!

WE CAN CALL IT A TOKEN OF APPRECIATION FOR MY OLD GOVERNESS.
UM...
ACTUALLY, THEY'RE ...

THERE'S NO PROBLEM AT ALL WITH IT!
......
??

THAT'S IT THEN!
PLEASE! YOU MUST ALLOW ME!

I NEED A LITTLE TIME TO THINK ABOUT IT.
OF COURSE!

I'M HOME.
WELCOME BACK.

OH? *REALLY?* DID YOU PERHAPS RUN ACROSS OUR *YOUNG MASTER JONES* IN THE STREET?

WHAT IS IT, EMMA?
OH. NOTHING ...

......

OH. SO YOU *DID*.
UH ...
... YES.

HE TOLD ME TO SAY HELLO TO YOU.
IS THAT RIGHT?

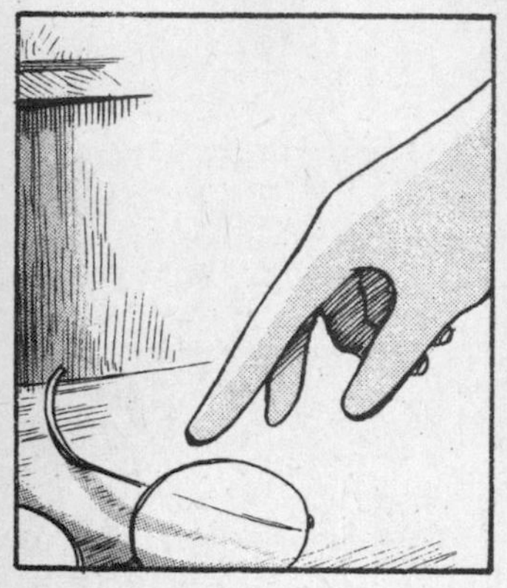

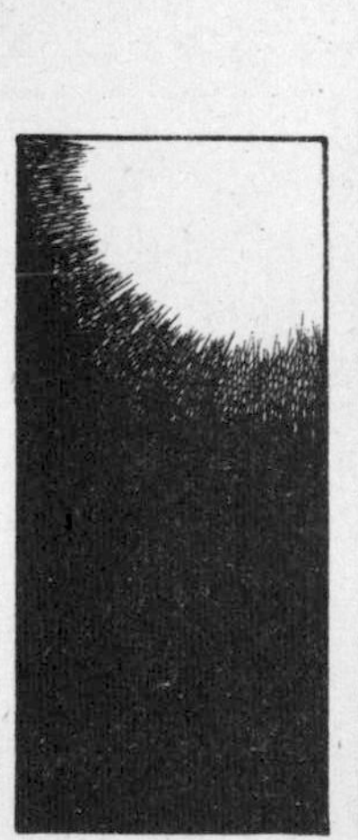

EMMA? WHAT HAPPENED?

KRSSHH

I'M SORRY.
I DIDN'T SEE IT THERE...

YOU BROKE ANOTHER ONE?

CAREFUL YOU DON'T CUT YOUR HANDS.

......

BY THE WAY...

...ABOUT THE STAIRS...
...SOMETIMES EVEN AFTER YOU CLEAN THEM, THERE'S STILL DUST IN THE CORNERS, SO DO A MORE THOROUGH JOB FROM NOW ON.

YES, MA'AM.

LOOK. IT'S RIGHT *THERE.*

TSK! THAT DOG WANDERS INTO MY YARD, EASY AS YOU PLEASE.
I WONDER WHOSE IT IS.

WOOF!
WOOF!

......

WELL...
DO THEY FIT?

TELL ME...
ARE YOUR EYES *BAD?*

THEY MAY FEEL STRANGE UNTIL YOU GET USED TO THEM...

THE BIRDS ...

THEY'RE FINE.

... ARE BRIL-LIANT.

I DIDN'T KNOW ...

... HOW BEAUTIFUL THE LAND-SCAPE WAS.

THAT'S RIGHT.

WHAT?
YOU DON'T NEED THEM?

BUT...
REALLY...

......

...I'M FINE...
...JUST LIKE THIS.

I'VE GOT IT!! WHAT WOULD YOU LIKE *INSTEAD?*
ANYTHING AT ALL, YOU NAME IT! THERE MUST BE *SOMETHING* YOU WANT!

I'M SORRY. I DO APPRECIATE THE THOUGHT ...
NO, NO, THAT'S ALL RIGHT.

...A LACE ...

WELL ...

SOME-THING ...?
YES, SOME-THING! ANY-THING!

A *HANDKER-CHIEF?* THEN SO IT SHALL BE!! I'LL GET YOU *100, 200* OF THEM!
UH, NO ...
...JUST *ONE* WOULD BE PERFECT.

...A LACE HANDKER-CHIEF WOULD BE NICE...

......

LACE HAS BEEN MY DREAM, FROM WHEN I WAS LITTLE...
LACE? REAL-LY?

THANK YOU, MR. JONES.
NOT AT ALL...

Chapter Two: The End

EMMA ...
EMMA?

WHERE ARE YOU?

YES? I'M RIGHT HERE.
OH, THERE YOU ARE.

I'M LOOKING FOR A THIMBLE ...

LOOK!!

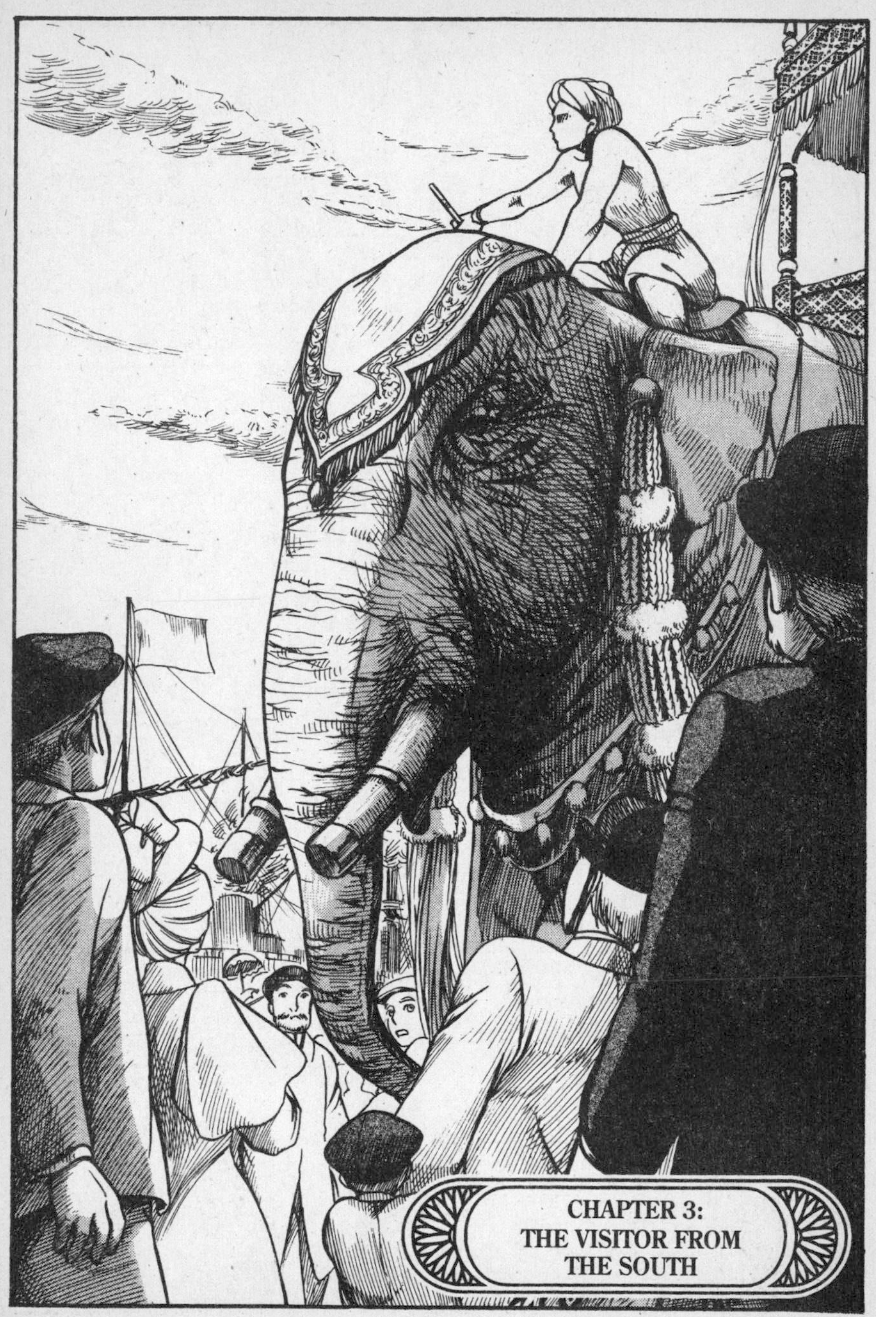
CHAPTER 3:
THE VISITOR FROM
THE SOUTH

THE ABOVE IS LAST MONTH'S SALES...

...AND HERE IS THIS MONTH'S PURCHASING LIST.
FINE.

WHEN ARE THE GOODS DUE TO ARRIVE BY STEAMER?

B-R-R-R-I-N-N-G
THEY SHOULD HAVE BEEN HERE BY NOW. I'LL INQUIRE ONCE AGAIN.

KA-CHA
TELL THEM TO GET IT HERE AS SOON AS POSSIBLE.

IF THOSE PACKAGES AREN'T DELIVERED, BUSINESS CANNOT GET DONE!

WE'VE GOT EMPTY STORE SHELVES HERE JUST WAITING ON THEIR MERCHAN-DISE.

TAP TAP TAP

UM...
...YOU HAVE *GUESTS*...

GOOD LORD!!
EXCUSE ME!!

...WAITING IN THE COURT-YARD.

CRIKEY!!
FWISH

BWAAAAAAA

SWISH
SWISH
SWISH

SWISH

LONG TIME NO SEE, WILLIAM.
HAS MY SUDDEN VISIT SURPRISED YOU?

HA...

HAKIM...

IN FACT, I'VE NEVER IMAGINED MY COURT-YARD LOOKING LIKE THIS.
IF YOU LIKE THEM, I COULD SPARE YOU ONE. GO AHEAD, PICK ANY ONE YOU FANCY.

I HAD NO IDEA THAT YOU WOULD BRING A HERD OF *ELEPHANTS* ...
PWAAAA

IT'S JUST MY GRANDMOTHER AND HER CONSTANT NAGGING...
IT MAKES ME WANT TO GET OUT AND TRAVEL BY MYSELF.

I'LL PASS, THANK YOU.
NOW, WHAT BRINGS YOU HERE SO SUD-DENLY?
OH, NOTHING SPECIAL.

BY YOUR-SELF.

...SO I THOUGHT IT WOULDN'T HURT TO CALL ON YOU FOR ONCE.

AT FIRST SIGHT, I THOUGHT YOU INTENDED TO *MOVE* HERE.
YOU'VE ALWAYS VISITED ME BEFORE...

WELL, I DON'T MIND YOU HOLIDAYING HERE...

...BUT WHAT ABOUT THEM?
IF THOSE BEHEMOTHS SHOULD GO INTO A RAGE...

YOU HAVE NOTHING TO WORRY ABOUT ON THAT ACCOUNT.

PWAAAA
RUN AWAY!
OR YOU'LL BE TRAMPLED!
ELE-PHANTS CERTAINLY HAVE LARGE FRAMES...
...BUT THEY ARE BY AND LARGE, MEEK, TRANQUIL CREATURES.
WHOA!
IT MOVED!!

AFTER ALL, THEY ARE *INTELLIGENT*, SACRED ANIMALS.
CRUSH

THWACK
ASSAULT-ING HUMANS IS A *RARITY*.

THEN HOW DO YOU EXPLAIN *THAT* RUCKUS?
AAAH!
AAAH!
OH, PAY NO ATTENTION. THAT ONE JUST HAS A SHORT FUSE.
BUZZ BUZZ
BUZZ

!
!

ELE-
PHANTS
IN MY
COURTYARD
FOR ONE
WEEK...
ONE
THING
...

ANYWAY,
I SHALL
ACCEPT YOUR
HOSPITALITY
FOR A MERE
WEEK.

...ONE
WEEK?!
FEAR
NOT. I'VE
BROUGHT
ALONG
MOST OF
MY OWN
NECESSITIES.

OH, YES!
I'M
TRAVELING
INCOGNITO,
SO NOT A
WORD ABOUT
MY VISIT
TO
ANYONE.

LOADING
THE
ELEPHANTS UP
WAS NO
PROBLEM, BUT
WE'LL NEED
A FEW MORE
HANDS TO HELP
US UNLOAD
THEM.
YOUR
SERVANTS
SHALL DO
FINE.

MASTER
WILLIAM...
WELL,
IT CAN'T
BE HELPED,
I SUPPOSE.
HELP THEM
WITH THEIR
LUGGAGE.

"PRINCE HAKIM ATAWALLY, OF THE ATAWALLY ROYAL FAMILY OF INDIA, IS STAYING AT THE JONES ESTATE WHILST TRAVELING INCOGNITO IN LONDON..."

HMF...

AND HE'S FROM... *INDIA?*
YES. THE ATAWALLY FAMILY ALSO ENGAGES IN TRADE.
THEY MOST LIKELY SHARE A BUSINESS CONNECTION.

THAT FAMILY HAS MORE WORLDLY ACQUAINTANCES THAN ONE MIGHT THINK...
...THOUGH THE VERY IDEA OF TRAVELING "INCOGNITO" IS SHATTERED ONCE ITS PUBLISHED IN THE PAPERS.

INDIA...

I WONDER IF THEY RIDE ELEPHANTS?
OH, PLEASE!!

HOW CAN HE EXPECT TO TRAVEL UNDERCOVER WHEN HE'S GOT PACHYDERMS PARADING THROUGH TOWN?!

INCOG-NITO? ALL OF LONDON KNOWS!

NOK NOK NOK
MASTER WILLIAM?

MASTER HAKIM IS WAITING FOR YOU IN THE COURTYARD.
THE COURT-YARD?

WHAT'S WRONG?
COME ON, WHAT ARE YOU WAITING FOR? HOP ON!

ON... ON AN ELE-PHANT ...?
ACTUALLY, NO ONE'S SUPPOSED TO RIDE THEM BUT ME, BUT YOU'RE A SPECIAL CASE!

EH?

MY COVER IS ALREADY BLOWN, SO WE MIGHT AS WELL GIVE THE PEOPLE SOMETHING TO LOOK AT!

LET'S RIDE!

WH...?

GULP

IS IT PICADILLY CIRCUS COME TO TOWN?
THE LONDON ZOO, MORE LIKE!

... WHAT THE?
AN ELE-PHANT?

WELL, WHAT DO YOU THINK? EVEN BACK IN INDIA, NO ONE HAS THE CHANCE TO GET A VIEW LIKE THIS, FROM ATOP AN ELEPHANT!
TRUE, I CERTAINLY DON'T GET TO SEE THE CITY FROM A VANTAGE POINT LIKE *THIS* EVERY DAY...

WE'RE A PERFECT *SPECTACLE*...

IF IT WEREN'T FOR THIS ROCKING...
I'M JUST HAPPY YOU'RE ENJOYING YOURSELF.

WHOA!

डषम्रोगर.
FULL SPEED AHEAD!

OH, YES! SHALL I SHOW YOU WHAT HE CAN DO?
WHAT'S THAT?

!!
WH UMP
WH UMP
WH UMP
WH UMP

W-WAIT !!
RUNNING MAKES THE...

EH?!

... WORSE !!

... EVEN ...

... SHAKING ...

!!
WH UMP
WH UMP
WH UMP
WH UMP
WH UMP

THIS IS THE *FASTEST* OF ALL MY ELEPHANTS!

MR. JONES?

HA...
HAKIM...
STOP...
STOP THE ELEPHANT...

YOU'LL PROBABLY FEEL A LITTLE BETTER IF YOU VOMIT...
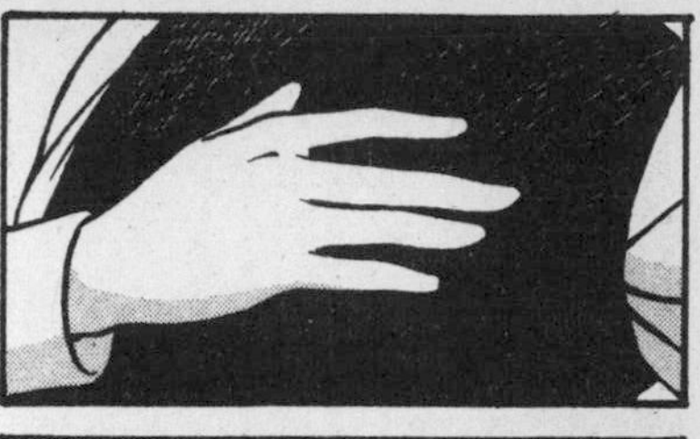

ARE YOU ALL RIGHT?

WHO KNEW ELEPHANTS WERE SO SHAKY ON TOP?

SHAMEFUL! A GROWN MAN WITH MOTION SICKNESS!
MAN WASN'T MEANT TO RIDE THOSE BEASTS!

...NO IDEA ...

YOU'RE PERSPIR-ING A GREAT DEAL.

I HAD...

AT FIRST, I HAD NO IDEA WHAT THAT WAS CHARGING DOWN THE STREET.

DO YOU FEEL *BETTER* NOW?
YES. *MUCH.*

DO YOU REALIZE, THE ONLY WAY YOU COME HERE IS *SUDDENLY?*
I'M SORRY.

WELL, IT ISN'T YOUR FAULT TODAY...

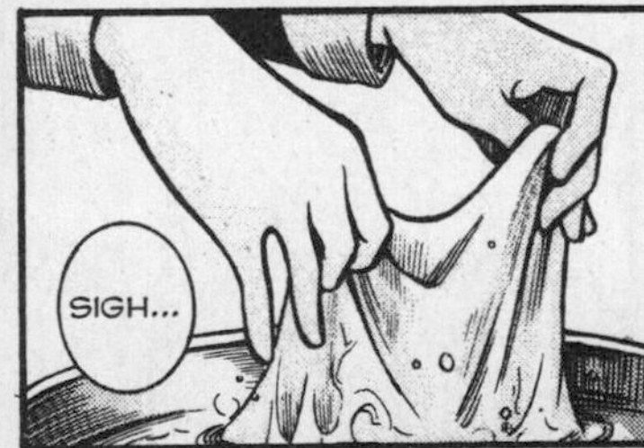
SIGH...

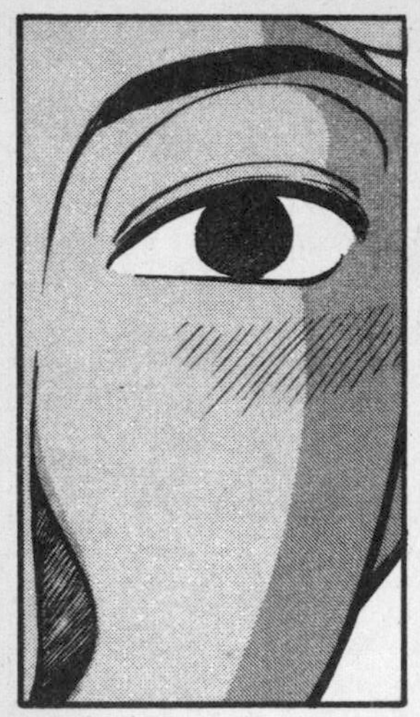

THIS IS HAKIM.
HE'S HOLIDAYING IN LONDON.

......
HELLO.

?

EMMA?
YES, MA'AM.

EMMA...

?

I'M SORRY TO HAVE DROPPED IN UNANNOUNCED.
GIVE MY REGARDS TO YOUR FATHER.

THANK YOU.
BE CAREFUL.

......

...WHAT'S WRONG, HAKIM? YOU'RE UNCHARACTER-ISTICALLY QUIET.
DO YOU HAVE MOTION SICKNESS, TOO?
......

YOU KNOW, WHEN WE FIRST STARTED, OUT I WAS PETRIFIED...
...BUT ONCE YOU GET USED TO IT, IT'S NOT ALL THAT BAD.
And I got to see Miss Emma again.

BUT PERHAPS IT WOULD BE BETTER TO GO DOWN A STREET WITH LESS PEDESTRIAN TRAFFIC...

...AND *THESE* ARE FOR *YOU*.

THESE WOULD BE FOR YOUR MISTRESS...

?

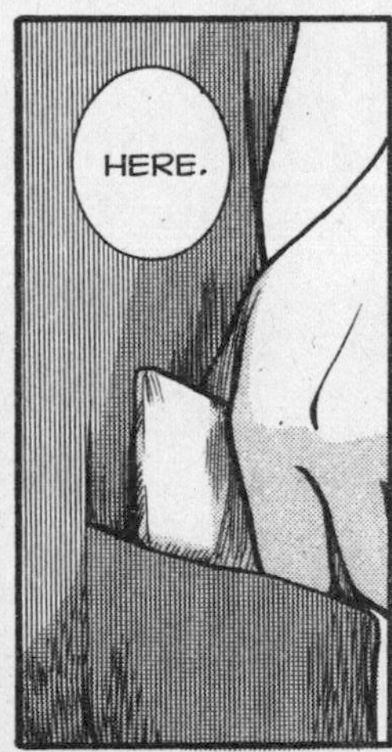
HERE.

THANK YOU...
AND I'VE GOT A SPECIAL DELIVERY AS WELL.

CHAPTER 4: THE LOVE LETTERS

THE MAIL?

AN IMPRES-SIVE AMOUNT, AS ALWAYS.

I WOULD BE HAPPY IF JUST *ONE* OF YOUR GENTLEMEN WOULD SEND *ME* A LETTER, TOO!
AH-HA-HA!
MADAM ...

IT MEANS THAT THE MERCHANDISE YOU ORDERED IS READY AND HAS BEEN DELIVERED.

"WILBUR AND HOPKINS"...
WILBUR & HOPKINS
LONDON,
STREET. 48
WHAT DOES IT MEAN?

......

THE GENTLEMAN IS WAITING FOR YOU IN THE PARLOR.
INDEED.
WELL. WHERE IS IT?

I DON'T RECALL PLACING AN ORDER WITH THIS COMPANY.
Buying so much these days, it slipped my mind.

THANK YOU VERY MUCH FOR YOUR PATRONAGE, SIR.

WOULD YOU CARE TO EXAMINE THE PIECE, SIR?

HUM.

HERE IT IS.

NAME?

IS THE NAME CORRECT?
MMM...

BELOVED, EMMA

AH... SURELY...
THE ORDER WAS PLACED BY SOMEONE IN THE JONES HOUSEHOLD.

COULD I SEE THAT?
OF COURSE.

EMMA...
WHAT?!

......
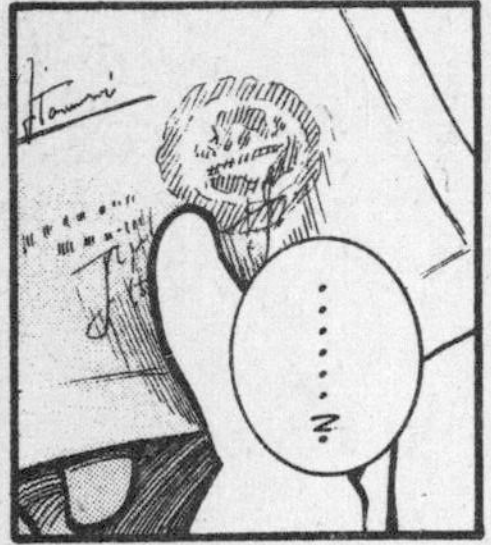
......?

......
CERTAINLY, THIS IS...

...HAKIM?!
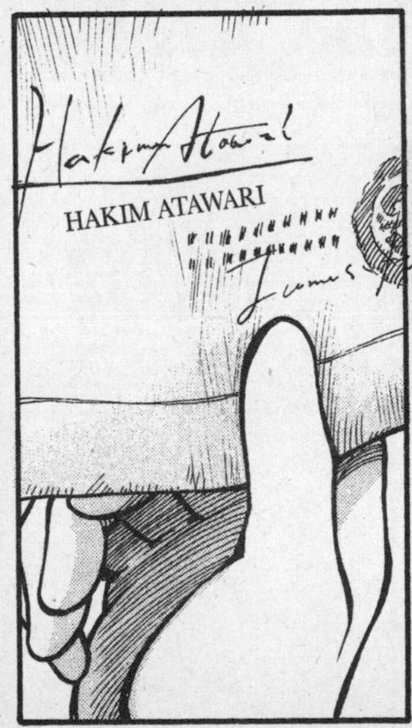
HAKIM ATAWARI

NOW THAT I THINK ABOUT IT, NOTHING HAS PROGRESSED SINCE THE LAST TIME I WAS HERE.
MISS EMMA AND I ARE STILL LITTLE BETTER THAN PERFECT STRAN...

WHAT'S *HE* DOING HERE?! AND IN THOSE CLOTHES?!
FOR THAT MATTER, WHAT AM *I* DOING HIDING?!

HAKIM ?!

?

PLEASE, COME IN.

...

I NOTICED YOU'RE NOT ACCOMPANIED BY MR. JONES TODAY.

I BELIEVE MY LADY SHALL RETURN SOON.
PLEASE HAVE A SEAT.

I DON'T KNOW IF THIS SUITS YOUR TASTE, BUT...

CLATTER

......

ACTUALLY ...

...I CAME HERE TO SEE YOU.

EMMA, ARE YOU WILLIAM'S BELOVED?
EH?!
...NO.
NOTHING OF THE KIND.

IF YOU WERE, THAT WOULD PUT ME IN A BIND.

GOOD.

FOR WILLIAM IS ONE OF MY FEW TRUSTED FRIENDS.
AND AS MUCH AS POSSIBLE, I WISH TO BE FAITHFUL TO HIM.

...AND I DON'T WANT TO CAUSE YOU ANY TROUBLE...
...BUT YOU SEE...

EMMA, I KNOW THAT WE HAVE JUST MET AND THIS IS RATHER SUDDEN...

...I AM IN *LOVE* WITH YOU.

TRUE, I DON'T KNOW MUCH ABOUT YOU.
I LIKE THE WAY YOU STAND. I LIKE THE WAY YOU MOVE.
I LIKE THE WAY YOU SPEAK SLOWLY.
AND YOUR VOICE, NOT TOO HIGH...
...BUT MOST OF ALL, I LIKE YOUR FACE.

......
MY FACE?

YOU DON'T *LIKE* YOUR OWN FACE?

......

I'VE BEEN THROUGH A LOT...

THAT CAN'T BE HELPED.
IT DOESN'T BOTHER ME A BIT.

HOW-EVER, EMMA...
...IF YOU HAVE NO OBJEC-TIONS...

...I INTEND TO PROTECT YOU FROM ALL HARDSHIPS FROM NOW ON.

...WELL, TELLING YOU THAT IS ONE REASON I CAME HERE TODAY.

MAINLY, THOUGH, I JUST WANTED A CHANCE TO SEE YOU AGAIN.
EVEN IF IT'S FOR THE LAST TIME.

...

WELCOME!

...ARE YOU LOOKING FOR A GIFT?

UM, NO, I...

THIS IS ONE OF OUR MOST *POPULAR* ITEMS.

IT'S MADE IN FRANCE, SO IT'S A *PERFECT* PRESENT FOR THE LADIES.
AND THE GENTLEMEN HAVE BEEN CHOOSING THIS.

IS THERE A MESSAGE?
EH? ER, YES...

BELOVED. EMMA
"BELOVED..."

NO, NO, NO, "EMMA..."
GIGGLE

?
EXCUSE ME.
I SHOULDN'T LAUGH.

I DON'T MEAN TO BE RUDE, BUT YOU'RE THE *FOURTH* CUSTOMER I'VE HAD WITH THAT REQUEST.

I'M ENVIOUS OF THIS "EMMA" PERSON.
ACTUALLY, I'VE CHANGED MY MIND.

EH?! B-BUT, SIR...!

...WILLIAM, OLD CHAP!!
FANCY SEEING YOU HERE!
HULLO.

WHERE HAVE YOU BEEN KEEPING YOURSELF THESE DAYS?
OH, HERE AND THERE.

AS USUAL YOUR ANSWER CRIES OUT FOR DETAIL.

?
WHAT IS IT? HAS SOMETHING HAPPENED?
NO.
NOTHING ESPECIALLY.

IT'S EMMA, ISN'T IT?

I KNOW! THE GIRL'S A BEAUTY!
BUT BEAUTIFUL OR NOT, SHE'S A *MAID!*
WHAT DIFFERENCE DOES IT MAKE?
FOR ME, THE GIRL AT THE LEYTON SHOP...
HE WAS SPURNED BY HER, TOO. THOUGHT BECAUSE SHE WAS QUIET, SHE COULDN'T RESIST HIS "CHARM."
OH, I'M SURE SHE FOUND HIM RESISTIBLE.
OY, EASE UP, LADS.

BUT ESPECIALLY NOT FROM SOMEONE WITH A LOW INCOME AND SOCIAL STATUS LIKE *YOU*, EH?
EMMA'S NOT THAT KIND OF GIRL!!

THE FACT IS, THAT GIRL WON'T ACCEPT ANY MAN'S PLEA.
I LIKE...

......

ALL RIGHT, CALM DOWN... YOU'RE OBVIOUSLY STILL SMARTING OVER IT.
YES, AS FOR ME, I FANCY THE LEYTON SHOPGIRL...

AREN'T YOU SLEEPING YET?

I HAVE TO ANSWER THESE LETTERS...

EVEN REJECTING ISN'T EASY, IS IT?
WHEN I TAUGHT YOU HOW TO READ AND WRITE, I NEVER IMAGINED THEY WOULD PROVE USEFUL TO YOU IN THIS FASHION.

YOU TURN THEM ALL DOWN, DON'T YOU?

......

WELL, THAT'S ALL RIGHT. DO AS YOU LIKE.
YES, MA'AM.
AS LONG AS IT DOESN'T AFFECT YOUR WORK TOMOR-ROW.

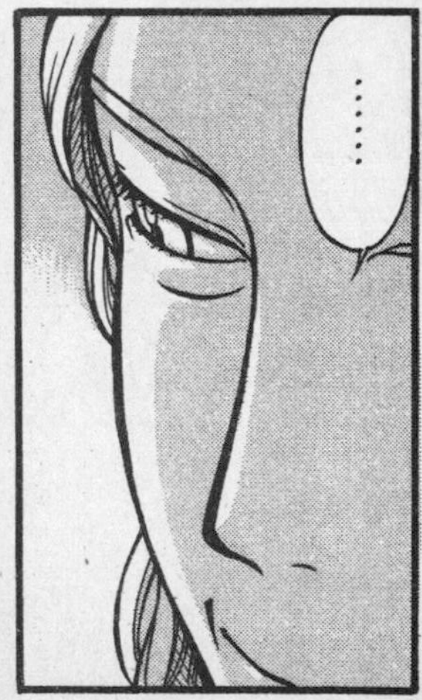
......

AND WHAT ABOUT YOU...
YOUNG MASTER?

Chapter Four: The End

IS THERE A MES-SAGE?
YES, THERE'S THIS FETCHING SHOPGIRL NAMED SARAH WHO WORKS AT LEYTON'S.

YES, OF COURSE.
GOOD.
AND FOR *YOU* AS WELL.

THIS IS ONE OF OUR MOST POPULAR ITEMS.
LEYTON
IT'S A *PERFECT* PRESENT FOR THE LADIES.

"THERE'S A RESTAURANT ON ST. JAMES STREET...
...AT THE HOTEL MEDAILLE.

MY MESSAGE TO HER IS...

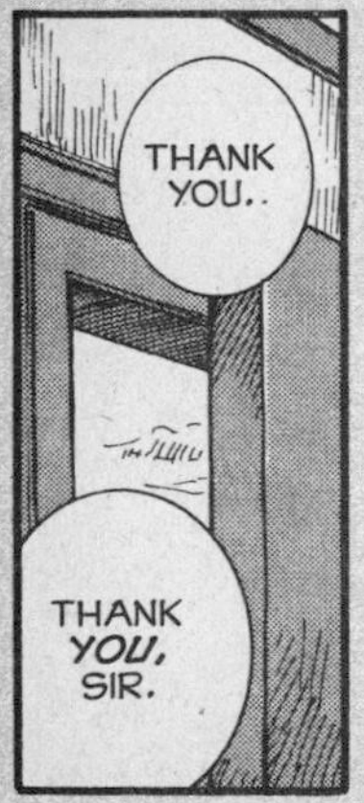
THANK YOU..
THANK *YOU*, SIR.

YES, I'LL GIVE HER YOUR MESSAGE.

I WOULD LIKE TO HAVE DINNER WITH YOU THERE."
...WOULD YOU PASS THAT ALONG?

YOU HAVE TO KEEP PERFECTLY *STILL* OR IT WON'T COME OUT!
THIS IS A GOOD DEAL MORE *STRENUOUS* THAN I THOUGHT.
YES, WELL, IT TAKES TIME.

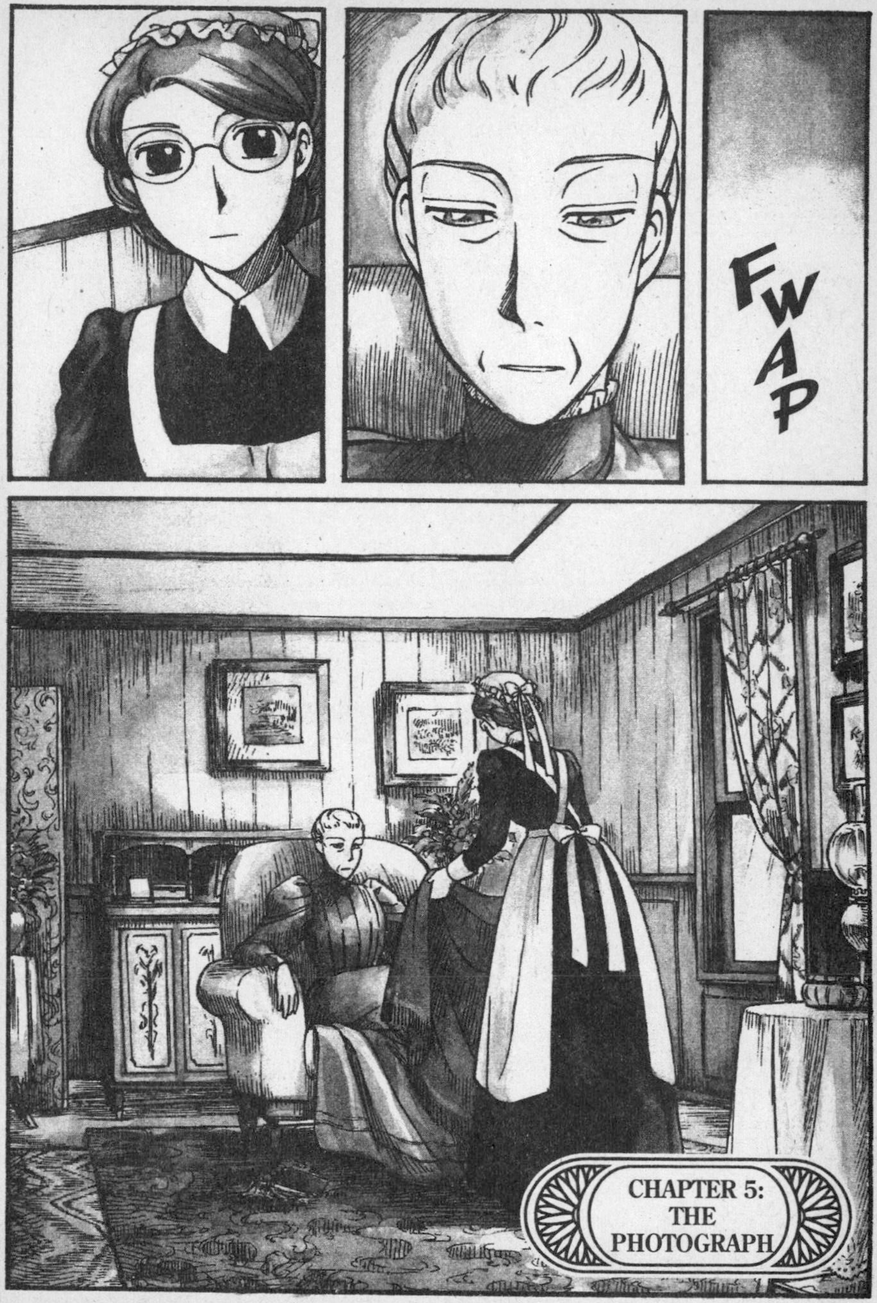

CHAPTER 5:
THE
PHOTOGRAPH

OH...
I MUST
HAVE
DRIFTED
OFF.

I HAD
A
DREAM.

A
DREAM?
YES.

...BUT
IT'S GONE
NOW. I
CAN'T
REMEM-
BER.

I BELIEVE
IT WAS
ABOUT
SOMETHING
A *LONG*
TIME
AGO...
......

MY NAME IS KELLY STOWNAR.
IT'S GETTING *CHILLY* IN HERE. LIGHT THE FIRE, WOULD YOU?
YES, MA'AM.

I MARRIED WHEN I WAS 18. AT 20, I BECAME A WIDOW.
I HAVE NO CHILDREN.

AFTER MY HUSBAND DIED, I WORKED AS A GOVERNESS FOR OVER 30 YEARS.

NOW RETIRED, I LIVE WITH MY MAID, EMMA.

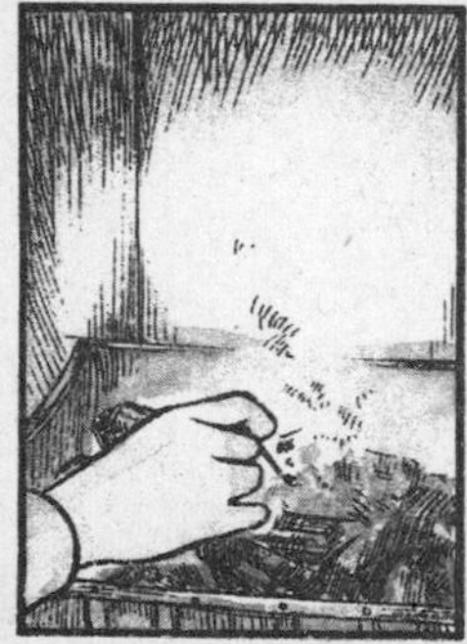

IF I HAVE ANY CONCERNS... WELL...
...THEY'RE ABOUT WHAT WILL HAPPEN TO HER AFTER I'M GONE.

SHE'S A GOOD GIRL.

IF SHE WOULD GET MARRIED, THAT WOULD PUT MY MIND AT EASE.

YES?
MMM...

SHE'S YOUNG, SHE'S BEAUTIFUL, SHE'S A HARD WORKER...IF SHE WERE JUST A TAD LESS MEEK, SHE COULD HAVE ANY NUMBER OF SUITORS...
...BUT THE THING ABOUT EMMA IS THAT SHE DOESN'T CARE A FIG ABOUT THAT.

I WONDER IF ANYTHING HAS HAPPENED BETWEEN THEM AFTER THAT DAY.
SHE HASN'T SWIFTLY REJECTED HIM LIKE ALL THE OTHERS, MEANING...SHE FINDS HIM SUITABLE, PERHAPS?

BUT WHAT ABOUT YOUNG MASTER JONES?
I HAD FORGOTTEN ABOUT HIM.

......

I WISH THE YOUNG MASTER WOULD ACT MORE LIKE A RESPONSIBLE ADULT, BUT AGEWISE, THEY'RE PERFECT FOR EACH OTHER.
NO, MY ONLY WORRY WOULD BE ABOUT HIS *FAMILY*.

SINCE WHEN DID I BECOME SUCH A MEDDLE-SOME OLD WOMAN? IS IT BECAUSE OF MY AGE?

IT'S RAINING.

OH...

INDEED IT IS.
WE'VE HAD QUITE A *LOT* OF IT RECENTLY.

WHAT DO YOU SAY TO THIS?!

LOUSE BEAR
E-BEAR

HO-HO!

ARE YOU SURE IT'S ALL RIGHT FOR YE TO BE LOAFIN' ALL DAY WITH US? WHAT ABOUT YOUR WORK?
AH, *BOLLOCKS* TO WORK!

OUTSIDE THE THREE A'US, NOT A SOUL KNOWS THAT I'M...
... HERE!
BLAST!

BRIIIING

BRINNNG

EH?

HELLO? "LOOSE AND BEAR!"

YEAH, HE'S HERE! HOLD ON A MINUTE, WILLYA?

......
YAH?

FOR ME?

IT'S THE MISSUS ...

AS MY HOUSE IS BECOMING WATER-LOGGED, I WOULD HAZARD A GUESS THAT THE DOWNPIPE IS BUSTED!

HELLO, AL! IT'S ME!!

I EXPECT TO SEE YOU HERE IN FIVE MINUTES!!
CLICK

I NEED YOU TO REPAIR IT, SO LEAVE RIGHT THIS MINUTE!!
THE WAY THIS IS GOING, WE'LL BE KNEE-DEEP IN NO TIME!

...I'VE BEEN SUMMONED.
TELL HER I'M NOT A RECEPTIONIST.

BUT THIS HOUSE IS STARTING TO GET RICKETY IN PLACES.
WELL, THAT CAN'T BE HELPED. IT'S OLD.
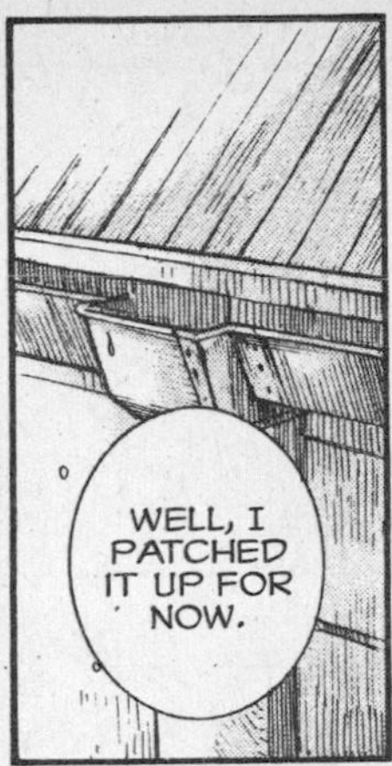
WELL, I PATCHED IT UP FOR NOW.

I THINK THE WALL-PAPER NEEDS TO BE REPLACED.
EVEN WHEN IT DRIES OUT?

JUST LIKE ITS OWNER, EH?
IMPUDENT RASCAL!

WELL, I'M GOING HOME. GIVE ME A HOLLER IF YOU NEED ME.
WAIT JUST *ONE* MOMENT.

IT'S PROBABLY GOING TO LEAVE WATER STAINS BEHIND.
I SEE... THIS WILL TAKE SOME WORK.
FIRST OF ALL, LET'S MOVE EVERY-THING OUT OF THE WAY...

YOU WOULDN'T LET TWO WOMEN MOVE ALL OF THIS BY THEMSELVES, WOULD YOU?

I'M SURE SHE WAS A HANDFUL FOR DOUG, TOO.

THAT KELLY'S BEEN MY SLAVE DRIVER SINCE *WAY* BACK.

HEAVE-HO!
BAM

...WELL, SURE. WE LIVED IN THE SAME NEIGBOR-HOOD.

DID YOU KNOW HER HUSBAND?

WHEN WE WERE BRATS, WE ALWAYS USED TO NICK APPLES FROM COVENT GARDEN, STUFF LIKE THAT...

SHE DOESN'T TALK TO YOU ABOUT "OLD TIMES?"
NO, NEVER... ALL I KNOW IS THAT HER HUSBAND PASSED AWAY.

SO YOU WERE...

HMPH.
WELL, I GUESS T'AIN'T A SUBJECT THAT'D BE MUCH FUN TO DREDGE UP.

......

WHAT'S THAT?
ER, I MEAN...

...ACTUALLY, I WAS WONDERING WHERE THEY MET.

...FRIENDS WITH BOTH MY LADY AND HER *HUSBAND*?

... REALLY?
THAT'S HOW IT WAS FOR EVERYONE BACK IN THE DAY.

OH, THE *USUAL* WAY. THE PARENTS' DECISION.
THREE MEETINGS AND THEN THE WEDDING IS THE WAY IT USUALLY WORKED.

WELL, YOU WOULDN'T, BECAUSE KELLY IS SO STUBBORN.

I NEVER IMAGINED ...

THE TABLE IN THE CORNER, TOO, PLEASE.
YEAH, YEAH.

WHO IS WHAT?
AH...

I'LL BE DOWN-STAIRS.
YES, MA'AM.

MADAM?!

THUMP
THUMP
THUMP
THUNK
AH!

WELL, I REALLY DID IT *THIS* TIME.
I SUPPOSE IT SERVES ME RIGHT.
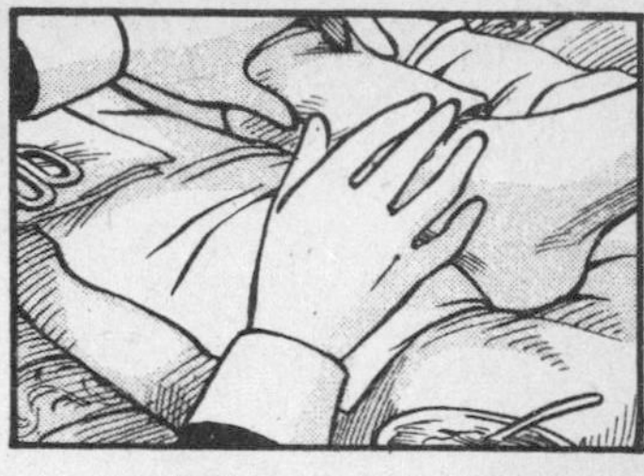

I WAS SO BUSY CARRYING THINGS THAT I WASN'T PAYING ATTENTION TO MY FOOTING.

THE STAIRS MUST BE LITTERED WITH THE DEBRIS FROM MY FALL.
I'LL CLEAN IT UP NOW.

SHE JUST ASKED ABOUT DOUG, SO I TOLD HER.

AL, YOU WERE TALKING TO EMMA BEFORE, WEREN'T YOU?
I HOPE YOU WEREN'T TELLING TALES OUT OF SCHOOL.

I SEE.

EMMA ASKED ...?

I BELIEVE IT'S A NECK-LACE.
I THINK I COLLECTED ALL OF THE PIECES BUT...

WHAT IS *THAT*?

....

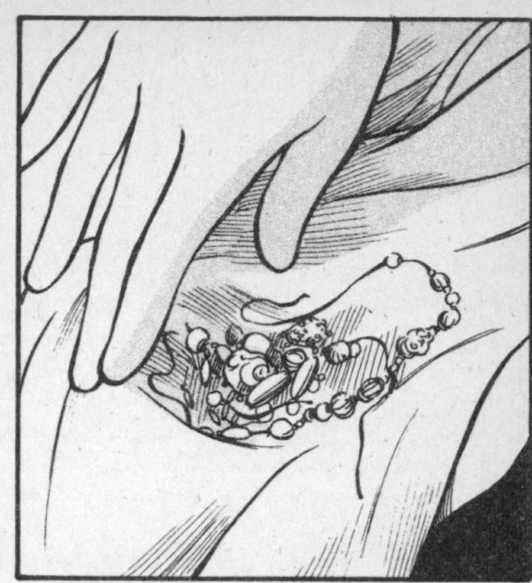

......
THE STRING MUST HAVE BROKEN.

...I DON'T KNOW HOW...
...TO PUT IT BACK TOGE-THER.

UNLUCKY DAY.
THOROUGH-LY.

AH, WELL. PUT IT AWAY AS IS.
YES, MA'AM.

WHEN IT RAINS, IT POURS.

YOU LIKE THE RAIN?
NO, I DESPISE THE RAIN ITSELF. LIKE IT WHEN THE RAIN STOPS.
IT FEELS SOMEHOW REFRESH-ING, DON'T YOU THINK?
NO, I FIND DURING AND AFTER THE RAIN TO BE QUITE UNPLEAS-ANT. TOO DAMP BY HALF.

WELL, YES, CERTAINLY...

SHALL I CHANGE THE BANDAGES, MADAM?
OH, YES. GO AHEAD.

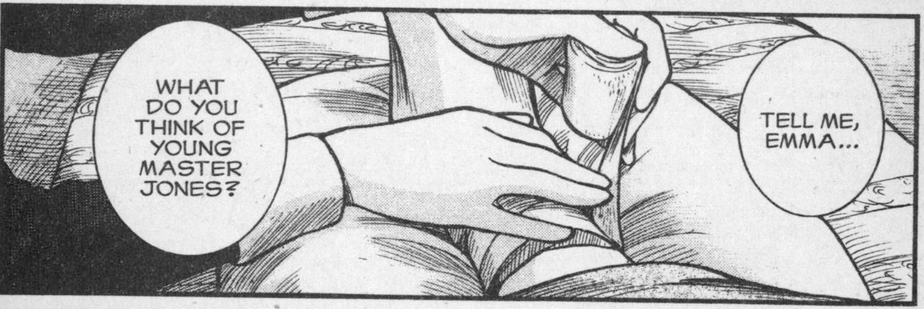
TELL ME, EMMA...
WHAT DO YOU THINK OF YOUNG MASTER JONES?

......

DO YOU INTEND TO TURN *HIM* DOWN, TOO?

MMM, YES...
Actually, not much in this world seems to bother him...

HE'S UNUSUAL.
HIGH-BORN AND YET, IT DOESN'T BOTHER HIM AT ALL THAT I'M A MAID.

HE HASN'T GIVEN ME THE STANDARD "YES/NO" CHOICE AS THE OTHERS HAVE.
HE JUST SEEMS TO...TAKE PLEASURE IN CONVERSING WITH ME.

AND DO YOU LOVE HIM?

......

I SEE.

MADAM ...

HERE...

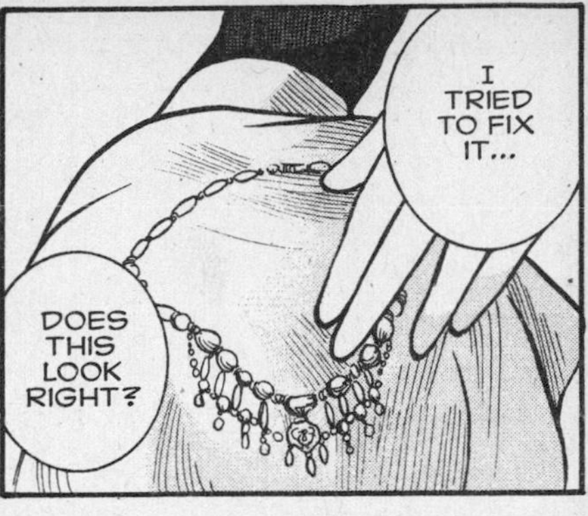
I TRIED TO FIX IT...
DOES THIS LOOK RIGHT?

... GOOD AS NEW.
HOW DID YOU KNOW?
I FOUND THIS PHOTO-GRAPH.

....

THIS MAN IS YOUR HUSBAND, ISN'T HE? THIS IS THE FIRST TIME I'VE SEEN HIM.

YES.
WHEN HE WAS STILL ALIVE.

I'LL PUT THE NECKLACE BACK IN YOUR ROOM.
THANK YOU.

THE PHOTO WAS TAKEN RIGHT AFTER WE HAD GOTTEN MARRIED.

I NEVER DREAM.
CURIOUS...

COME TO THINK OF IT...

PERHAPS HE CAME TO TELL ME TO GET A MOVE ON, TO BE BY HIS SIDE...

...I BELIEVE IT WAS *HE* WHO APPEARED IN THAT DREAM I HAD.

Chapter Five: The End

EH, IT'LL MAKE A NICE KEEP-SAKE.

SO YOU TOOK A PICTURE, EH?

WE HAD TO STAY STILL FOR THE LONGEST TIME.
MY SHOULDERS ARE STIFF.
KELLY'S A BEAUTY, IN'T SHE?
DOES A MAN SAY THAT ABOUT HIS OWN WIFE?

OH, DEAR. WE'RE OUT OF SUGAR.

SAY... AL, GO OUT AND BUY SOME MORE.
ME?
ASK DOUG HERE!

DOUG IS MY HUS-BAND.
I CANNOT HAVE HIM RUNNING ERRANDS.

NOW LEAVE AT ONCE!
SLAVE DRIVER!

ASHES TO ASHES, DUST TO DUST.

AMEN.
CHAPTER 6:
THE TWO CLOCKS

THE PHOTO WAS TAKEN RIGHT AFTER WE HAD GOTTEN MARRIED.
COME TO THINK OF IT...
...I BELIEVE IT WAS HE WHO APPEARED IN THAT DREAM I HAD.
PEOPLE SURROUND THEMSELVES WITH PHOTOS AND MEMENTOES OF THEIR LOST LOVED ONES...
PERHAPS HE CAME TO TELL ME TO GET A MOVE ON, TO BE BY HIS SIDE...

SAY, WHAT DO YOU MAKE OF OUR INDIAN GUEST?
I FIND HIM ATTRACTIVE, DON'T YOU?

I THINK HE JUST HAS A DIFFERENT PERSPECTIVE, COMING FROM ROYALTY, LIKE THAT.
IF WE'RE TALKING ABOUT UPPER CLASS, I WOULD TAKE MASTER WILLIAM OVER HIM ANY DAY OF THE WEEK.
WHAT ARE YOU TWO GOING ON ABOUT?
WHY JUST THE OTHER DAY...

NOT ME...
I THINK HE'S A RATHER ODD DUCK.
OH, REALLY?

RRRRRRR
YOU CAN GOSSIP ALL YOU WANT ON YOUR *BREAK*...
...MY LITTLE SKY-LARKS...

ALL RIGHT, THAT'S ENOUGH CHIT-CHAT!
AH!
CLAP CLAP

RRR

ROOOOOAARR
...BUT WHILE YOU'RE ON DUTY...

DID I JUST IMAGINE ...
RRR
...A MOTORCAR DRIVING DOWN THE HALLWAY?

YOU HAVE TO ADMIT, THIS PLACE HAS BECOME MORE EXCITING SINCE HE ARRIVED.
MORE LIKE *ECCENTRIC* ...

ZOOOOOM

ZOOOOOM
HEY, WILLIAM!!
SKREEE
......
NOW WHAT...?!

THIS IS A WONDERFUL TOY! IT DOESN'T EVEN NEED HORSES TO RUN!

OH?
YES, BUT IT'S MADE TO RUN *OUTDOORS*, NOT IN THE HOUSE.
And how did you get it up the stairs, anyway?

WEREN'T YOU SUPPOSED TO GO HOME AFTER ONE WEEK?
IT'S BEEN A LOT LONGER THAN *THAT*.

I'VE CHANGED MY MIND.
ENGLAND HOLDS *MANY* AMUSEMENTS FOR ME!

......

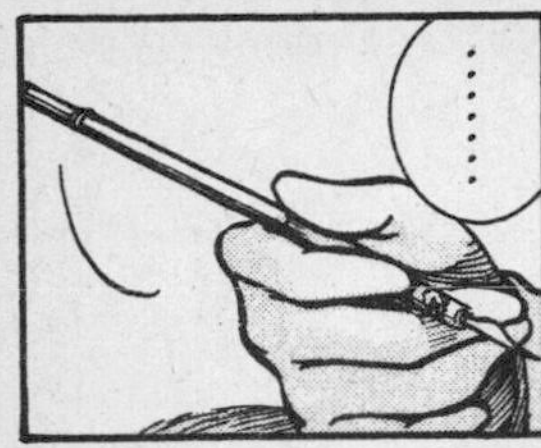
......

BY THE WAY, HAKIM, I'VE BEEN MEANING TO ASK YOU...

COME, LET US RIDE!!
EH?!

RIDE WHERE?!
OUTSIDE, OF COURSE, AS YOU SAID!

......
Well, good.
VRRRR

KRIK
KRIK

TIK
TOK
TIK
TOK

...IS THAT YOUR HUSBAND'S POCKET-WATCH?
THAT'S RIGHT.

ONE OF MY CHORES...
...USED TO BE WINDING IT PRECISELY 15 TIMES EACH MORNING.
FOR SOME REASON, I'VE KEPT IT UP EVER SINCE.

OF COURSE, NOW IT'S JUST A HABIT.
IN FACT, I'VE WOUND IT FAR MORE TIMES *AFTER* IT STOPPED BEING USED.

...
DID *YOU* MAKE THAT?
YES.

WON'T YOU EAT, EVEN JUST A LITTLE BIT?

I'M NOT VERY HUNGRY.

STILL, I THINK YOU OUGHT TO EAT...
...EVEN IF...EVEN IF JUST A SPOON-FUL.

ALL RIGHT, JUST THIS THEN.

I'VE GOT A FAVOR TO ASK.
YES?

...OH, YES.

NOTHING IMPORT-ANT.
JUST AN ERRAND.

NO, SIR. THIS DOESN'T LOOK GOOD.

DID YOU NOT CHECK IT BEFORE YOU LEFT?
IS IT BROKEN?

WHAT IS THIS "PETROL" YOU SPEAK OF?

HAKIM, YOU DIDN'T *KNOW* YOU WERE RUNNING OUT OF PETROL?

NO, YOU'RE OUT OF PETROL.
PETROL...

HOW ABOUT TAKING A CAR-RIAGE?
NO, I DIDN'T BRING ANY MONEY WITH ME.
WILLIAM!

WELL, IF YOU WAIT HERE, I'LL GO AND FETCH SOMEONE.
SLAM
OH, THAT'LL TAKE TOO LONG!

AH, THAT'S MUDIE'S.
"MUDIE'S?"

MM?
WHAT IS THAT OVER THERE?
WHERE PEOPLE ARE ENTER-ING?

......
BOOKS?

A LENDING LIBRARY.
I CAN'T RECALL, HAKIM. DO YOU READ BOOKS?

WHAT ARE YOU GOING TO DO? LEAVE THIS CONTRAP-TION HERE?!

LET'S GO THEN!
WAIT A MINUTE! I DON'T THINK YOU UNDER-STAND.

WE'LL BE BACK TO PICK IT UP LATER!!

HA-HA...

BUT...

UDIE'S
CT LIBRARY
IMITED

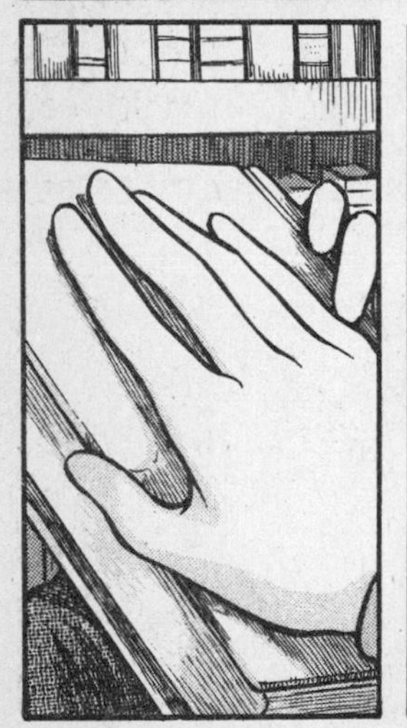

YOU SIMPLY MUST READ THIS.
AH!
IT'S A MARVELOUS STORY...

WAIT A MOMENT.

...ABOUT A MISTAKEN ROMANCE BETWEEN AN UNLUCKY, POOR GIRL...
...AND A NOBLE-MAN.

......

YOUR MEMBERSHIP CARD, PLEASE.

LET ME SEE...
THAT'S THREE BOOKS ALTOGETHER.

...IS MY LADY'S. I'M HERE AS HER PROXY.

EH?
BUT THIS NAME...

UMMM... KELLY STOWNAR...

AH, NOW I SEE.
I DIDN'T *THINK* SHE WAS THAT YOUNG.

Mademoiselle Cocotte
HAKIM! WHAT ARE YOU LOOKING AT?

WILLIAM, LOOK AT THIS!
IT'S ALL PHOTOGRAPHS OF WOMEN!
MM?

WHERE DID YOU FIND SUCH A THING?
RIGHT OVER THERE.

SO THAT'S WHAT KIND OF BOOK IT IS, EH?
HMPH. I SEE.

......

HUH. IS THIS ALL?
Boring...
THAT'S BECAUSE WHERE YOU COME FROM PEOPLE ALWAYS STRIDE AROUND HALF-NAKED...
FLIP FLIP FLIP

WHAT DO YOU THINK OF THIS ONE?
MM?

I PREFER THIS ONE MYSELF...
WHICH?

YES, SHE'S A GOOD ONE.
THAT'S WHAT I SAID.

YES, I NOTICED THAT I HADN'T SEEN YOUR LADY RECENTLY.
SO HER LEGS HAVE GONE BAD, EH? TSK-TSK.

BUT ONCE HIS LEGS GAVE OUT ON HIM, IT WAS ALL OVER, JUST LIKE THAT.

THAT'S A *SHAME*.
A LONG WAYS BACK, MY OWN FATHER NEARLY DROWNED IN THE THAMES BUT CAME OUT OF IT AS FIT AS A FIDDLE, AS IF HE COULDN'T DIE.

GIVE YOUR LADY MY BEST.
AND TAKE CARE OF HER.
THANK YOU.

SIGN HERE.

YES, I REMEMBER IT WELL.
IS THAT RIGHT?

AND AFTER THAT, THE LIBRARY WAS MADE OFF LIMITS.

?

HMM, NOW THAT YOU REMIND ME, I DO REMEMBER SOMETHING OF THE SORT TAKING PLACE...
...BUT THAT WAS SO LONG AGO, I'VE FORGOTTEN...

HAKIM?

OH.

THAT IS...
WHY...

FWAP
EH?!
WHAT ...?!

......
WERE YOU ON YOUR WAY OUT?

I MEAN, I NEVER THOUGHT I WOULD RUN INTO *YOU* HERE!

OH, YES! I'LL SEE YOU HOME...
AH! DRAT! I CAN'T LEAVE THE MOTOR-CAR.

ER, WELL, I SUPPOSE THAT'S THAT...
...'TIL WE MEET AGAIN.

ENOUGH OF THIS. LET'S CHECK OUT OUR BOOKS AND GO HOME.
COME ON, HAKIM.

...
HAAAA...

EH? I JUST SAW YOU TALKING TO THE YOUNG WOMAN, YES?

WILLIAM!! AREN'T YOU GOING TO TAKE *THIS* ONE?!
I HAVE NO INTENTION OF TAKING *THAT ONE* HOME, NUMB-SKULL!!

BUZZ
BUZZ
BUZZ
BUZZ
Numb-skull...?!

WHAT?

POOR THING. YOU SEE, THE LADY OF HER HOUSE...

AH! THAT'S ...
... KELLY'S GIRL.

MM?

SHE'S RUNNING. LORD, SHE'S YOUNG.

YOU'VE GOT EAGLE EYES.
WHERE?

...FOR THIS WORLD ALLOWS YOU NO MORE THAN A CUPFUL OF DREAMS. SO BE STINGY WITH YOUR TIME.. AND RUN.
OR SOMETHING LIKE THAT.
WHO SAID THAT, GOETHE?
NO, ME.

RUN, RUN, YOUNG ONE...

"IF YOU STOP WALKING...
...IT MEANS YOUR DAY OF REST IS NEAR."
At the end of the 19th century, in England...
...the averaage life span was 50 years.

Chapter Six: The End

NO, I'M AFRAID THERE'S NONE OF THAT AROUND HERE.
MMM... I THOUGHT NOT.

WHAT'S THAT?
SAYS HE'S LOOKING FOR OIL FOR HIS MOTORCAR.
BUT I CAN'T THINK OF A SINGLE SHOP 'ROUND HERE THAT SELLS THAT KINDA STUFF.

OIL?
NOT FOR ME. A YOUNG NOBLE-MAN.
HE RAN OUT OF PETROL, SO HIS MOTOR-CAR'S STALLED.

HAHA! RAN OUT OF PETROL!
JUST GOES TO SHOW THAT EVEN ARISTOCRATS AREN'T STRANGERS TO FOOL-ISHNESS.

WELL. THERE'S NOTHING FOR IT. I'D BETTER LOOK FOR A CART.
GO RIGHT AHEAD.
TAKE CARE A' YOUR-SELF.

FOOLISH ARISTO-CRAT, HM...?
HUH?
SOUNDS LIKE THAT "YOUNG MASTER" KELLY WAS TALKING ABOUT.

NO-THING.
NOT IMPOR-TANT.

Johann Strauss II

FRÜHLINGSSTIMMEN

Op.410

CHAPTER 7:
THE FATHER, RICHARD JONES

BUT SOON AS IT FLED, HE DREW A BEAD AND FIRED ONE SHOT!
BLAM!!

AND IT TOOK FIVE DOGS TO DRIVE IT OUT OF ITS HOLE.

HIS SKILL AS A HORSEMAN IS A GIVEN, BUT HE'S ALSO FIRST-RATE WITH RIFLES.
THERE ISN'T A FOX AROUND THAT HAS CAUGHT HIS EYE AND ESCAPED TO TELL ABOUT IT.

...MY, MEN DO LOVE TO TALK ABOUT HUNTING.
IT APPEARS YOU ARE *BORING* THE LADIES, OLD CHAP.

DO YOU ENJOY LAMBS-GATE?
YES, I OFTEN HOLIDAY THERE IN THE SUMMER.

BY THE WAY, DID YOU KNOW THAT A NEW STORE HAS OPENED ON REGENT STREET?
IT'S A MARVEL-OUS STORE.
WHY, YES! I SHOPPED THERE THE OTHER DAY.
THEY USE FRENCH DESIGNERS.

BY ALL MEANS, PLEASE COME IF YOU ARE FREE.
YOUR VERY PRESENCE BRIGHTENS UP ANY ROOM.
IT WOULD BE AN HONOR, MADAM.

IN FACT, NEXT TIME, I BELIEVE I SHALL GIVE A RECITAL AT OUR HOUSE THERE.
HOW LOVELY!

WHEN DID YOU ARRIVE?
A FEW MINUTES AGO.

AND WHO HAVE YOU GREETED?
JUST THE HOSTS.

SO YOU ACTUALLY SHOWED UP.
FOR THE TIME BEING.

LORD, IT FEELS LIKE YOU HAVEN'T SHOWN YOUR FACE IN AGES.
SO WHAT'S THE OCCASION?

MY FATHER COLLARED ME...

THE INVITATIONS THAT YOU'VE DECLINED.

I'VE HEARD FROM STEPHENS HERE THAT...
... RECENTLY, YOU'VE TURNED DOWN ALMOST ALL OF THE INVITATIONS YOU'VE GOTTEN.

STEPHENS, YOU HAVE NOTHING TO BE SORRY FOR.

MY APOLOGIES, SIR.

QUITE THE CONTRARY IT APPEARS THAT YOU HAD STEPHENS DO ALL THE DECLINING *FOR YOU.*
... TRUE.

PERHAPS IT'S BECAUSE YOU'RE YOUNG, BUT YOU LACK BASIC UNDER-STANDING OF THE *NECESSITY* OF SOCIAL CONTACTS.

...I'M SORRY. THERE WERE JUST SO MANY OF THEM...

BECAUSE OF OUR FORTUNE?
WELL, THAT, TOO.

WITHOUT ANY CLAIM TO NOBILITY, THE JONES FAMILY, A FAMILY OF MERCHANTS, IS ACCEPTABLE AMONG THE GENTRY AS ONE OF ITS OWN.
WHY DO YOU SUPPOSE THAT IS?

AND THE BEST PLACE TO CLEARLY EXPRESS THESE ELE- MENTS...
...IS IN FASHION- ABLE SOCIETY.

BUT THERE ARE THREE ELEMENTS EVEN MORE CRITICAL THAN THAT.
NAMELY, GRACE, INTELLECT AND DECORUM.

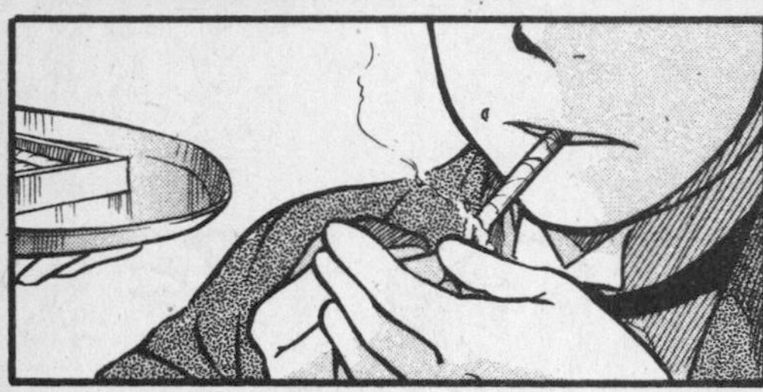

FIRST FASHION- ABLE SOCIETY IS MADE UP OF THE ARISTO- CRACY.
SURELY, EVEN YOU REALIZE THAT MUCH.

THIS, TOO, IS BUSI- NESS.
STRICTLY SPEAKING, YOU SHOULD ACCEPT *EVERY* INVITATION YOU RECEIVE.

BUT...
...WITH HAKIM VISITING ...

TAKE HIM WITH YOU.
IT WOULDN'T HURT HIM EITHER TO GET ACQUAINTED WITH FASHIONABLE SOCIETY IN THIS COUNTRY.

ARE YOU HERE ALONE?
NO.

MY FRIEND IS OVER THERE, SHEPHERDING THE BELLE OF THE BALL ACROSS THE ROOM.

HUH. SO HE'S *YOUR* FRIEND, IS HE?

WITH HIS NEW FACE AND APPARENT ABILITY TO STAND OUT IN A CROWD, HE'S GOT ALL THE LADIES' TOUNGUES WAGGING. SPECULATION IS RUNNING RAMPANT AS TO HIS INDENTITY.
"TO THE MANOR BORN."
THIS SETTING IS HIS FORTE.

HIS FORTE, EH?
IT'S NOT ESPECIALLY UP MY ALLEY.

WELL, BE AS IT THAT AS IT MAY, IT DOES US NO GOOD STANDING LIKE STATUES.

10

OURS IS TO MEET, GREET, MAKE THE ROUNDS, DANCE A WALTZ OR TWO...
...IS IT NOT?
SO I'VE BEEN TOLD...

...BUT TO BE PERFECTLY HONEST...
...I FIND IT ALL VERY TIRESOME.
THEN WHY BOTHER COMING?

MR. WILLIAM JONES?

IT'S BEEN TOO LONG MADAM.
GOOD EVENING.
FAR TOO LONG.
OH, YOU'RE HERE TOO, ROBERT.

I HADN'T SEEN YOU FOR SO LONG, I THOUGHT PERHAPS YOU HAD TAKEN ILL...
NO, NO. NOTHING LIKE *THAT*...

ARE YOUR FATHER AND MOTHER WELL?
YES, I WOULD VENTURE TO SAY THEY'RE STILL ENJOYING GOOD HEALTH AND CLEVER MINDS.

WHO MIGHT THIS FINE LADY BE?
MY DAUGHTER.
ELEANOR, INTRODUCE YOURSELF.

I KNEW I SHOULD HAVE WORN MY LACE GLOVES.
ARE YOU STILL PRATTLING ABOUT THAT?

THIS IS HER FIRST BALL.
WELL, WELL.

SHE DOESN'T LIKE HER DRESS, SHE DOESN'T LIKE HER HAIRSTYLE. I DON'T KNOW HOW MANY TIMES SHE MADE ME FIX IT!
MOTHER!!

MR. JONES, WOULD YOU DO ME THE HONOR OF DANCING ONE WALTZ WITH MY DAUGHTER?

...THE HONOR IS MINE.

BUZZ
BUZZ

GOOD AFTERNOON.
WELL, HELLO! WHAT CAN I DO FOR YOU TODAY?

DO YOU HAVE ANY ASPARAGUS?
YEP. JUST GOT SOME IN LAST NIGHT.

AH! IT'S MISS EMMA!!
ENMA!!

GOOD AFTERNOON.
ARE YOU SHOPPING?
SOPPING?

KNOW WHAT? I'M GOING OFF TO BOARDING SCHOOL!
BOARD SCHOOL!

BOARDING SCHOOL?
YOU'RE NOT GOING!

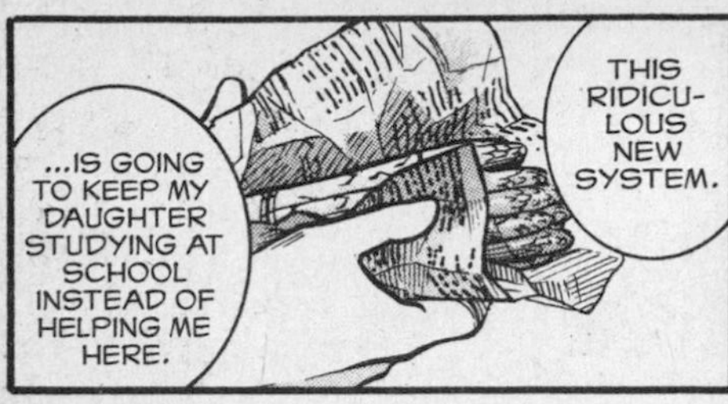
THIS RIDICULOUS NEW SYSTEM.
...IS GOING TO KEEP MY DAUGHTER STUDYING AT SCHOOL INSTEAD OF HELPING ME HERE.

PUBLIC ELEMENTARY SCHOOL.

WHO'LL WANT A BRIDE WITH A HEAD FULLA FACTS?

I THINK IT'S A FINE IDEA. AN EDUCATED LADY WILL BE THE FASHION, YOU WAIT AND SEE!
IF A GIRL CAN RECITE EVEN JUST ONE POEM FROM MEMORY...

...SHE COULD BECOME QUITE THE CATCH FOR A MARRIAGE-MINDED ARISTOCRAT.
SNORT
STUFF AND NONSENSE!

NOTHIN' COMES OF STUDYING!

THANK YOU AND COME AGAIN!
THANK YOU! COME AGAIN!
AG'IN!

BUZZ BUZZ

IT APPEARS THAT VEGETABLES HAVE BECOME SLIGHTLY CHEAPER THESE DAYS.
IS THAT SO?

WELCOME BACK.

OH, AND A LETTER CAME.
WELL, THE ENVELOPE IS CERTAINLY FANCY.

YOU'VE BEEN EATING NOTHING BUT PUDDING LATELY...
....AND I'VE BOUGHT ASPARAGUS, SO TODAY...
EMMA ...

IT APPEARS THAT I'M GOING TO BE PAID A SYMPATHY VISIT...
...BY JONES *PERE ET FILS.*

......

WELL, ACTUALLY, I DIDN'T HEAR IT STRAIGHT FROM THE SOURCE, SO...

IT'S *ABSURD!* WHY DIDN'T YOU INFORM ME OF SUCH IMPORTANT NEWS?

RATTLE
WHETHER THE INFORMATION COMES FIRST-HAND OR FROM THE GRAPEVINE, WHEN YOUR FORMER TEACHER IS ILL IN BED...
...YOU PAY HER A VISIT.
RATTLE

WILLIAM, YOU SIMPLY MUST BECOME MORE AWARE OF THE CONCEPT OF COURTESY.

YES, BUT I DON'T SEE WHY *YOU* HAVE TO GO AS WELL.
I'VE BEEN MEANING TO VISIT ANYWAY, SO THIS COMES AS PERFECT TIMING.

RATTLE
RATTLE
IT TOOK OVER *TEN YEARS* OF MY HARANGUING BEFORE YOU FINALLY SAW FIT TO CALL ON YOUR TEACHER.
......

PLEASE, COME IN.

HOW *KIND* OF YOU TO COME.
FORGIVE ME FOR NOT GETTING UP.
THAT'S QUITE ALL RIGHT, MRS. STOWNAR.

IT'S BEEN A LONG TIME, MR. JONES.
YOU HAVEN'T CHANGED A BIT.

AND YOU LOOK IN MUCH BETTER SPIRITS THAN I IMAGINED.

OH, I'VE ONLY INJURED MY LEG.
IT'S NOTHING ***SERIOUS***.

THAT'S VERY GRACIOUS OF YOU TO SAY SO.
SSS
IT MAY BE HIS NATURAL DISPOSITION, BUT HE'S ALWAYS BEEN A TAD, SHALL WE SAY, UNFOCUSED.

...OH, NO. THAT'S NOT TRUE. HE WAS A GOOD STUDENT.
HE WAS JUST SOMEWHAT EASILY DISTRACTED.
SSS

RIBIT

PERHAPS IT'S JUST HIS AGE.

IF I'VE SAID IT ONCE, I'VE SAID IT A HUNDRED TIMES, BUT THE BOY STILL LACKS SELF-AWARENESS.

...AS FOR ME...

I WOULD LIKE TO THINK SO, BUT...

AH...

......

AS FOR ME...
...I WOULD LIKE TO TURN OVER THE REINS OF THE JONES FAMILY BUSINESS SOON.

AT THE MOMENT, I'M HEALTHY AS A HORSE, YES.
BUT THERE MAY COME A DAY WHEN I BECOME DISABLED, LIKE YOU.

INDEED ...
...I INTENDED TO BE CAREFUL...

YES. THINKING OF YOUR *CHANCE* ACCIDENT FILLS ME WITH EVEN MORE UNEASINESS.

AS TO WILLIAM, I BELIEVE HIS CHARACTER MAY CHANGE FOR THE BETTER ONCE HE GETS MARRIED AND SETTLES DOWN.
LUCKILY, THAT SEEMS TO BE COMING TO A CONCLUSION.

......
OH.

YOU SEE, THERE'S A CERTAIN YOUNG LADY WHO IS VERY INTERESTED IN WILLIAM AND HAS READILY AGREED TO MARRY HIM.

THIS IS THE FIRST TIME I'VE HEARD ANYTHING ABOUT "MY MARRIAGE!"
BUT OF COURSE. THEY HAD TO DISCUSS THE MATTER WITH ME FIRST.

...HOLD UP!
WHAT ARE YOU *TALKING* ABOUT?

WHO IS IT?
THE GIRL YOU DANCED WITH AT THE BALL THE OTHER NIGHT. YOU SEEM TO LIKE HER, TOO.

WHA--

I DANCED WITH HER OUT OF *POLITE-NESS!!*
IT WOULD HAVE BEEN RUDE IF I HAD REFUSED!!

IT'S NOT 50 YEARS AGO, WHERE PARENTS OF TWO CHILDREN GET ALONG SO THEY ORDER THEIR OFFSPRING TO WED!
I WILL HAVE NO PART OF THIS, DO YOU UNDERSTAND ME?!

HAVE YOU *ANOTHER* GIRL IN MIND?

......

I ASSUME SHE IS A PROPER LADY, SUITABLE TO MARRY INTO THE JONES FAMILY?
......

...
I...
I...

EMMA ...

THAT YOUR PERSONAL FEELINGS FOR THE WOMAN ARE IMPORTANT IS BEYOND DISPUTE. HOWEVER...
... MARRIAGE BETWEEN TWO PEOPLE FROM THE SAME *COUNTRY* IS TO BE DESIRED.
OH, SHE'S NOT A FOREIGNER.

GREAT BRITAIN IS ONE, YET WITHIN IT ARE *TWO* COUNTRIES...

... CONSISTING OF THE GENTRY AND *ABOVE*... AND THOSE WHO ARE *BELOW*.

Chapter 7: The End

MR. JONES IS A PECULIAR GENTLE-MAN.

AND YET THESE DAYS, YOU CAN'T GET YOUR FILL OF TALKING ABOUT HIM.
IT SEEMS YOU REALLY DO FANCY HIM.

BUT HE SAYS HE DOESN'T REALLY ENJOY THE SOCIAL SEASON.
HE SAYS IT MAKES HIS STOMACH, FEET AND MOUTH TIRED.

OH, THAT'S NOT SO!
OH, BUT IT IS.

DO YOU REALLY THINK SO?
I KNOW SO.

......

MISS ELEANOR ...
...STOP SITTING CROSS-LEGGED.
AH!

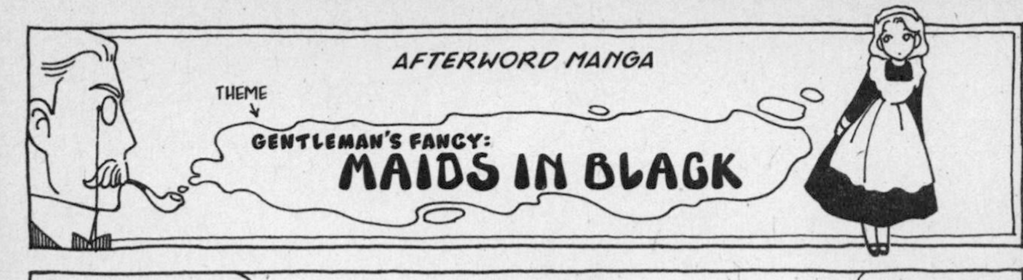

Holmes never had a moustache.

BUT SOMETIMES THIS HAPPENS AT OUR MEETINGS...

EMMA'S EMBARRASS FACE IS...
...THE MOST IMPORTANT THING OF ALL...
IT'S IMPORTANT!!
IMPORTANT!!
...TANT!!

SORRY.

AND SO I PRETTY MUCH GET TO DO WHAT I WANT. KELLY HAS AN ACCIDENT, DADDY APPEARS...

...BUT I THINK THE STORY IS STARTING TO MOVE FORWARD NOW.

STILL, I'VE GOT ALL KINDS OF IDEAS THAT'LL PROBABLY GET JAMMED INTO VOLUME 2.

I BOUGHT THE MARILYN MONROE DVD BOXED SET AND HAVE BEEN WATCHING LIKE A MONKEY EVERY SINGLE DAY.

Poo-poo-pee-doo♡

IF FATE ALLOWS, LET'S MEET AGAIN IN VOLUME 2!
SEE YOU THEN!

WILL EMMA AND WILLIAM'S RELATIONSHIP SURVIVE? FIND OUT IN DECEMBER.

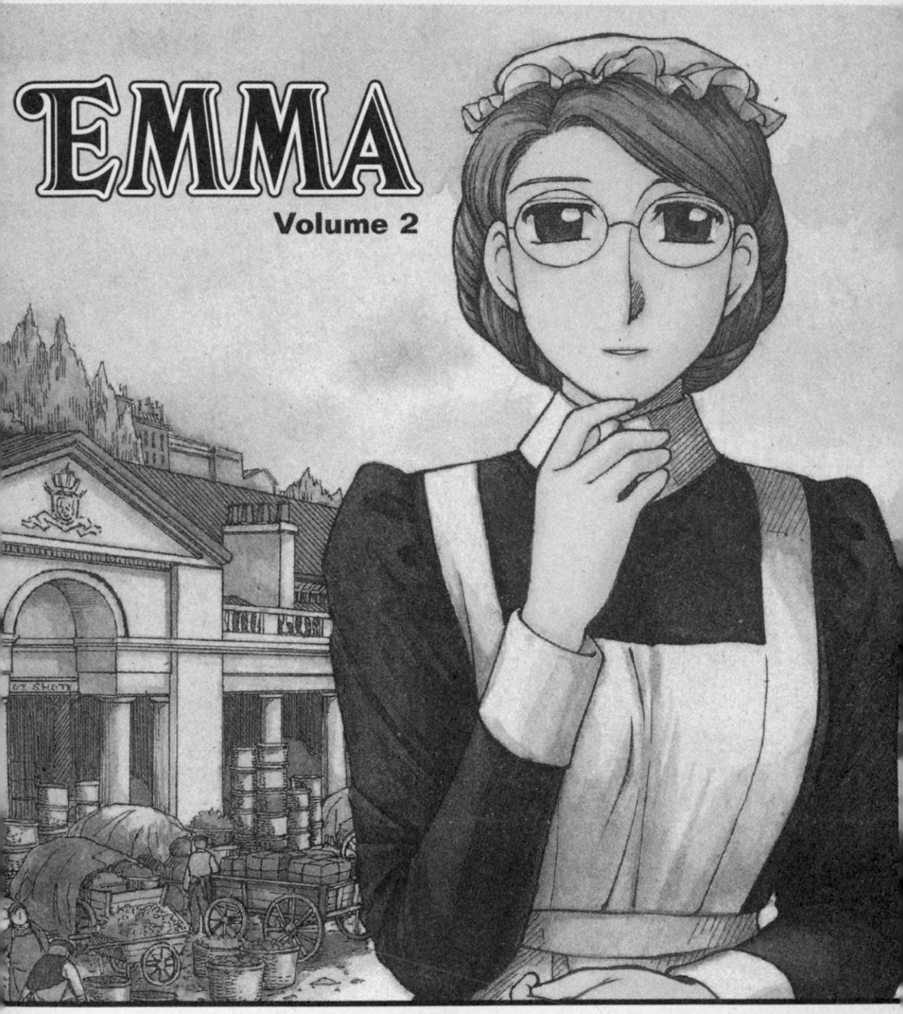

EMMA

Volume 2

By Kaoru Mori. After Emma and William's first real date, things seem to be going in a positive direction for them. But the leisurely pace of their growing relationship ends when tragedy strikes at home, forcing Emma to leave the house she shared with Mrs. Stownar. Meanwhile, when the rest of William's brothers and sisters show up, they discover their brother's budding relationship and try to bring it to a screeching halt.

Welcome to Emma's World

In Victorian London, as the end of the 19th century approached, picking yourself up by your own bootstraps and lifting yourself out of poverty wasn't really an option. Class defined your future, not your own ambition—sadly, it was even worse for women. For a girl not born into the upper classes and abandoned at an early age, prospects for the future were especially grim.

If you were that girl, what would happen if a kind-hearted woman—former governess to an aristocratic family—took you in? If she decided to take care of you and train you to become a proper British maid? A life of servitude may not seem glamorous to those of us living in today's world, but it would have been a great stroke of luck for someone trapped by poverty, someone whose other choices were the poorhouse or the slums of London. Of course, the lucky person in our story is Emma, the star of this series.

The Woman Behind EMMA

EMMA is the creation of Kaoru Mori, a relatively young mangaka (she's under 30) who harbors a real love for all things British, but particularly for the England of the Victorian era. It's hard to explain what attracts certain people to different cultures and time periods that are alien and far-removed from their own. But whatever the reason, Ms. Kaoru's passion comes through on every page.

She has carefully researched her material, and every illustration is meticulously drawn to create as accurate a depiction of London circa 1885 as possible. In fact, she even brought in an historical consultant to assure the series' accuracy. The kind of realistic art direction seen in the pages of EMMA is something that people are perhaps more accustomed to experiencing in cinema rather than comics. The total effect makes you feel that you are there with the characters in the world she has created (or recreated, as the case might be). There is nothing supernatural or fantasy-related about the adventures of EMMA. It's simply a lovingly rendered speculation on what it might have been like to live in London as a maid in that bygone era.

Ms. Kaoru has been publishing the serialized adventures of Emma in a Japanese monthly anthology called *Comic Beam* (Enterbrain) since 2002. In that short time, the series has captured an intensely loyal following, and a highly praised anime series was spun out from this manga. (As of this writing, the series is unavailable in America.) EMMA created something of a phenomenon in Japan and is said to have spawned an interest in English maid "cosplay" with fans dressing up in the attire of the series. We hope that we can help spread this kind of enthusiastic following to America as well.

EMMA just recently concluded its run in Japan in early 2006. We at CMX are excited to be presenting the collected, translated versions of EMMA in their entirety and un-retouched. We hope you will enjoy your journey back through time, as you follow the adventures of Emma, William, Kelly Stownar and all the other wonderful, three-dimensional characters from the mind of master storyteller Kaoru Mori.

Jim Chadwick

Jim Chadwick
CMX Editor

EMMA Volume 1, published by WildStorm Productions, an imprint of DC Comics, 888 Prospect St. #240, La Jolla, CA 92037. English Translation © 2006. All Rights Reserved. English translation rights in U.S.A. and Canada arranged by ENTERBRAIN,INC. through Tuttle-Mori Agency, Inc., Tokyo. The stories, characters, and incidents mentioned in this magazine are entirely fictional. Printed on recyclable paper. WildStorm does not read or accept unsolicited submissions of ideas, stories or artwork. Printed in Canada.

DC Comics, a Warner Bros. Entertainment Company.

Sheldon Drzka – Translation and Adaptation
Janice Chiang – Lettering
Larry Berry – Design
Jim Chadwick – Editor

ISBN:1-4012-1132-1
ISBN-13: 978-1-4012-1132-5

All the pages in this book were created—and are printed here—in Japanese RIGHT-to-LEFT format. No artwork has been reversed or altered, so you can read the stories the way the creators meant for them to be read.

FLIP IT!

RIGHT TO LEFT?!

Traditional Japanese manga starts at the upper right-hand corner, and moves right-to-left as it goes down the page. Follow this guide for an easy understanding.

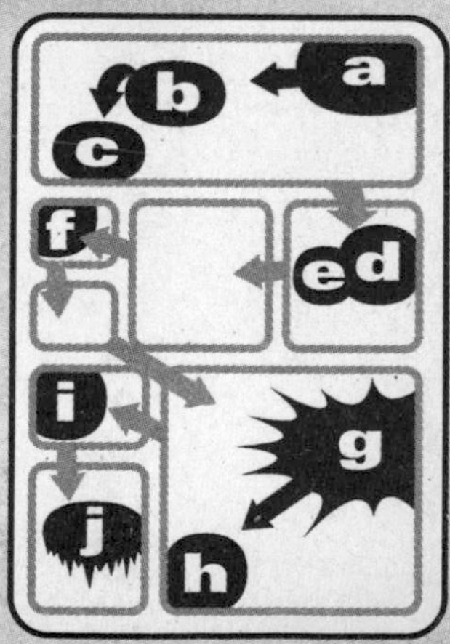